Teachers, School Boards, and Collective Bargaining: A Changing of the Guard

Robert E. Doherty

and

Walter E. Oberer

ILR Paperback No. 2

New York State School of Industrial and Labor Relations,
a Statutory College of the State University,
Cornell University, Ithaca

Copyright © 1967 by Cornell University
All rights reserved
Library of Congress Catalog Card number: 67–63482

1st Printing, 1967
2nd Printing, 1968

Price: $2.00

ORDER FROM:

Distribution Center, New York State School of Industrial and Labor Relations, Cornell University, Ithaca, N.Y. 14850

PRINTED IN THE UNITED STATES OF AMERICA
BY THE CAYUGA PRESS, INC.

Contents

Foreword

By a process not entirely unlike an unplanned pregnancy, a project which began as a modest holding of scholarly hands has blossomed into a book. As originally conceived, this study was to have been a bulletin in the School of Industrial and Labor Relations' series on current developments in employment relations. The verbosity of the authors produced a volume that transcended the "bulletin" category without quite measuring up to any other established literary form. The consequence is that their manuscript has been assigned to that miscellaneous reservoir of undisciplined pedantry — "book."

As such, it has been deemed deserving of the accoutrements befitting its genre. Accordingly, we make the following acknowledgements. To Professor Leonard Adams, Director of Publications, we express our gratitude for his staunch permissiveness in the face of our word barrage. To Professor Kurt Hanslowe, who read the manuscript more times than he would like to remember, we express our condolences. To Frances Eagan, for her deft editorial hand, we express our relief.

In this context, it is customary for authors to thank their wives for their patience, help, and inspiration. We are sorry to report that our standards of honesty will not permit us to do this. Indeed, once our wives learned that it was unlikely that the "book" would add any money to the family coffers or luster to the family names (two compensations they seem ever willing to share), their indifference approached hostility. We would, however, like to thank them for the small effort they made in helping to prepare the index — such as it is.

R. E. D.
W. E. O.

April 1967
Ithaca, New York

Introduction

An expert, according to an old and rather lame joke, is anyone with a briefcase who is more than twenty miles from home. By this standard, if no other, the authors of this volume qualify as experts in the new field of collective bargaining in public education. Both have picked up their briefcases and traveled on many occasions, one to serve as a moderator and arbitrator in teacher representation and bargaining disputes, the other to conduct conferences and workshops in employer-employee relations for board members, school administrators, and teachers.

To be sure, we have not been at these chores for long, although our involvement is almost as old as the problems themselves. When we first became interested in teacher-board of education relationships, there was but one school district, New York City, in which teachers were covered by a comprehensive agreement, and only one state, Wisconsin, had passed legislation providing for collective bargaining rights for public school employees. Now, two and one-half years later, there are statutes in seven other states providing for some sort of bargaining rights for teachers, and scores of comprehensive collective agreements have been negotiated.

This book was written during the summer of 1966. Thus our findings are based on very recent history, an era that educational historians of the future will likely call the seminal period of formal collective employment arrangements in education. It is almost as if someone had written a book about the nature and history of steamboating in 1811, just four years after Robert Fulton had launched the *Clermont*. Be that as it may, we think there is a need for a contribution at this time from those who have had experience in this area. In some states statutes have been enacted hurriedly, often with a bow toward one or the other of the contending parties — teacher organizations, administrators, and board members —

who are themselves groping, however pontifical their institutional stances, for suitable answers to the many questions involved. This small volume may serve as a faint beacon for those concerned with providing a more appropriate structure for teacher-school board relations in a time of somewhat chaotic, but creative, flux.

Our methodology, if we may use such an exalted term to describe the way we went about our task, was to reflect upon and compare our experiences "in the field," to study the relevant documents (agreements, salary schedules, statistical materials, statutes, opinions of courts, public agencies, and arbitrators, and the emerging speculations of scholars), to interview veterans of the young campaign hardly past its first skirmishes — in summary, to organize and share our experience, research, and thinking on the subject at hand. We have assumed that the questions that aroused our curiosity would hold similar intrigue for school officials, teachers, legislators, and that elusive character every writer tries to reach, the intelligent, public-spirited citizen.

There seemed to us four broad questions of fundamental importance: What has prompted this movement toward bilateral determination of employment conditions in public schools? What is the character of the teacher organizations behind this movement? What are the legal questions raised by collective action among teachers and what legislation has been and should be enacted? What implications does teacher bargaining have for the quality of the educational enterprise? The four chapters of this work constitute our effort to answer, seriatim, the foregoing questions.

The answers are not definitive. But the alternative to writing now on the basis of our present, tentative conclusions is to postpone the contribution we may be able to make until a time when life will have passed us by, when the relationships which are now in the process of jelling will have acquired a set beyond the reach of any guidelines, warnings, or caveats we might suggest. This is particularly the case with respect to Chapter 3, in which we assess and evaluate current teacher bargaining statutes and make our tentative recommendations. We have chosen to risk a premature judgment in preference to a delayed post-mortem. In short, we have stuck our necks out in order to get our noses into the problems involved while they are still viable.

I

The Public School Teacher as Employee

WHEN BENJAMIN FRANKLIN AND
his friend James Ralph had exhausted both funds and credit during
their first visit to London in 1725, Ralph, unable to find work as an
actor, copyist, or journalist, finally tried his hand as a schoolmaster in
Berkshire. "This, however, he deemed a business below him," Franklin
later wrote in his autobiography, "and confident of future better fortune,
when he should be unwilling to have it known that he once was so
meanly employed, he changed his name, and did me the honor to assume mine."[1]

It is not surprising that Ralph should want to keep his "mean employment" a public secret. The colonial society from which he and Franklin
had come, primarily agricultural and overwhelmingly pragmatic, at-
tached little importance to formal schooling. The low status it afforded
those it hired to instruct the young was but a reflection of this indifference. Teachers were often recruited from the lowest order. On the eve
of the American Revolution, Jonathan Boucher reported from Mary-
land: "Not a ship arrives either with redemptioners or convicts, in which
schoolmasters are not as regularly advertised for sale, as weavers, tailors,
or any other trade; with little other difference, that I can hear of,
excepting perhaps that the former do not usually fetch as good a price
as the latter."[2]

---

[1] Benjamin Franklin, *The Autobiography of Benjamin Franklin* (New York:
The Modern Library, 1960), p. 51.

[2] Jonathan Boucher, "A View of the Causes and Consequences of the American Revolution: In Thirteen Discourses, Preached in North America between the
Years 1763 and 1775," p. 184, as quoted in Howard K. Beale, *A History of Freedom of Teaching in American Schools* (New York: Charles Scribner's Sons,
1941), p. 11.

1

While a handful of these teachers performed creditably, the majority evidently did not. "It is a general plague and complaint of the whole land," a disgruntled colonist remarked, "that for one discreet and able teacher you shall find twenty ignorant and careless."[3] Nor were they free from other vices. Colonial schoolmasters, Willard Elsbree has observed, had a reputation for drunkenness, for financial misdemeanors, and for being runaways.[4] Even among the few who were of good character and diligent at their task, only a small number had an opportunity to learn their craft well. The average length of tenure of masters was short. In Dedham, Massachusetts, between the years 1654 and 1757, for example, it averaged one year and ten months.[5]

The coming of the nineteenth century brought about no significant improvements. Salaries remained miserably low, tenure was short, and the esteem with which teachers were held by the citizenry seemed to vacillate between contempt and indifference.

Salaries are as good an indication as any of how highly we value an individual's service. Between 1841 and 1860, salaries for rural men teachers rose from an average of $4.15 to $6.28 a week; salaries for rural women teachers were about two-thirds of this figure. Urban men teachers earned twice as much as did their counterparts in the countryside, while urban women teachers received only the same amount as rural men teachers. During the same period, Warren Burgess has estimated, the cost of living for a small family living a frugal life and consuming the same commodities over the entire period rose from $7.00 to $8.00 weekly.[6]

During the prosperous Civil War years, the average teacher's salary in California was $357. "Out of this annual average salary," the state school superintendent complained, "teachers must board and clothe themselves, and pay their income tax! An average servant girl receives three hundred dollars a year, *and her board*; an average farm hand gets the same; and even an able-bodied Chinaman gets three hundred dollars a year, boarding himself."[7] At about the same time, in Philadel-

---

[3] As quoted in Charles A. Beard and William G. Carr, "Colonial School Days," *The Journal of the National Education Association,* vol. 24, no. 2 (February 1935), p. 43.

[4] Willard Elsbree, *The American Teacher* (New York: American Book Company, 1939), pp. 17–31.

[5] *ibid.,* p. 81.

[6] Warren R. Burgess, *Trends of School Costs* (New York: Russell Sage Foundation, 1920), pp. 32, 54.

[7] California Department of Education, *Thirteenth Annual Report of the Superintendent of Public Instruction* (1863), p. 11, as quoted in Elsbree, p. 281.

phia, the board of controllers commented ruefully, "... A large portion of the teachers receive less than the janitress who sweeps the School-House."[8]

Somewhat earlier, Horace Mann had discovered in Massachusetts that, in "one of the most cultivated towns in the Commonwealth," all journeymen craftsmen had higher salaries than teachers — several received 50 percent more and a few had salaries that exceeded those of teachers by 100 percent. The simple and cruel facts, wrote Mann, are "... We pay best, 1st, those who destroy us, – generals; 2nd, those who cheat us, – politicians and quacks; 3rd, those who amuse us, – singers and dancers; and last of all those who instruct us, – teachers."[9]

One might argue that one of the chief reasons American education did not slip to such a depth that it became unsatisfactory even to the most educationally indifferent was that females were eventually allowed into the schools as teachers. Before 1830, there were few women teachers in the common schools. Teaching, from ancient times, had always been regarded as a masculine task. This tradition, coupled with the low status of women during the early national period, their relatively low educational level, and the general concern that females would be unable to discipline unruly students, tended to perpetuate masculine domination. Housewives had served as teachers in the so-called dame or infant schools during the colonial and early national period, teaching small children their ABC's and the rudiments of grammar. Later a few had been employed in the public schools teaching small children. But it was not until about the fifth decade after the Revolution that women began to take over the schoolmaster's role in significant numbers. The reasons for their recruitment were couched in principled terms: "Their manners are more mild and gentle, and hence more in consonance with the tenderness of childhood," as the 1841 report of the Boston Board of Education put it, and also females were "of purer morals"[10] — but more important, it seemed, was that a burgeoning economy had provided employment opportunities for apostate schoolmasters at salaries local taxpayers were unwilling to match.

The outbreak of the Civil War hastened the decline of male domination. In Indiana, the proportion of men teachers fell from 80 percent in 1859 to 59 percent in 1864; in Ohio, the ratio went from 52 to 41

---

[8] *Forty-sixth Annual Report* (Philadelphia, 1864), p. 31, as quoted in Elsbree, p. 281.

[9] *Common School Journal*, vol. 9 (1847), p. 367, as quoted in Elsbree, p. 280.
[10] Elsbree, p. 201.

percent in roughly the same period.[11] In state after state, male teachers became a minority as great numbers enlisted or were drafted for military service. Most did not return to the classroom after Appomattox. The percentage of female teachers increased thereafter, unevenly but steadily, until the late 1920's when it reached a peak of about 83 percent.[12]

Two other consequences of low teacher salaries during the nineteenth century (or were low salaries the consequence?) were a continually high turnover rate and a chronic problem of unqualified and inept teachers. Unquestionably, throughout most of the nineteenth century, teaching was regarded as one of the most casual of occupations. Of the 1,896 teachers in Connecticut in 1857, for example, only 348 had taught in the same school for two or more successive years. At the same time, over 60 percent of Pennsylvania's teachers had three years or less of teaching experience, while only 18 percent had taught more than six. The average length of service for Rhode Island teachers was two years. The state school superintendent in New York, two years earlier, had estimated that one-third of that state's teachers would quit at the end of the current school year. Replacements for departing teachers seem almost always to have been novices, young in age as well as in experience. In Pennsylvania, the average age of public school teachers in 1856 was twenty-three years, with nearly a third being under twenty-one. A decade later in Maine the average age was twenty-one.[13]

As one might expect, these teachers were hardly consumed by dedication to their craft or profession. Their motives for entering teaching in the first place evidently had little to do either with intellectual interests or a desire to serve children; as observed by the Vernon, Connecticut, board of school visitors in the late 1840's: "A young man busy in the summer, looks around in the fall to determine how he shall spend the winter months. He thinks of turning peddler, or of working at shoemaking. But the one will expose him to storms, the other he fears will injure his chest. He therefore concludes that although he can make more money in these or some similar employment, he will nevertheless teach school for a meager compensation."[14]

Out on the raw frontier, where there seemed to be even less concern than in New England about staffing the schools with teachers of reason-

[11] *ibid.,* p. 206.

[12] U. S. Department of Health, Education, and Welfare, *Statistical Summary of Education, 1957–58* (Washington: GPO, 1958), Bulletin no. OE-60003, p. 8.

[13] Elsbree, pp. 293–294.

[14] "Connecticut Board of Education, 1847," p. 48, as quoted in Elsbree, p. 280.

able competence, the quality and character of teachers were probably of a lower order. Westerners might have grudgingly admitted that there was some use for formal education, but it did not necessarily follow that teachers themselves were very important. "The man who was disabled to such an extent that he could not engage in manual labor," a product of a Midwestern school recollected, "who was lame, too fat, too feeble, had the phthisic or had fits or was too lazy to work — well, they usually made schoolmasters out of them."[15]

Teachers, then as now, were just about as good as their salary levels. It seems extraordinary that there were so many teachers of real talent and dedication in the nineteenth century — and, one might add, today as well — willing to work for a pittance when these same talents could easily have been put to use at more remunerative tasks. Nor should it be forgotten that, while there were many criticisms of teachers and the schools, to the great bulk of Americans, as De Tocqueville observed, the schools, such as they were, seemed to be harmonious with their temperament and adequate to their needs. "True information is mainly derived from experience," De Tocqueville wrote, and as for the Americans, ". . . book learning would not help them much at the present day."[16]

II

How does the contemporary American teacher compare with those discussed in the previous pages? Obviously, one finds noticeable improvements but they are improvements that have been tempered by nineteenth-century values that refuse to loosen their grasp. Teachers have not escaped history. They must cope with public attitudes toward education, including the willingness to pay for it, that are only slowly evolving toward generous support. In short, teachers have not arrived as doctors, lawyers, and architects have arrived: professionally, in income, or in public esteem.

Yet the prestige of the teacher is probably higher today than ever before. When the National Opinion Research Center asked a "representative" group of Americans in 1947 to rank ninety occupations as having an excellent, good, below average, or poor standing, 26 percent thought the standing of teachers was excellent, 45 percent thought good, and 24 percent thought average. Only 3 percent thought the standing below

---

[15] R. Carlyle Buley, *The Old Northwest* (Indianapolis: Indiana Historical Society, 1950) vol. 2, p. 370.

[16] Alexis De Tocqueville, *Democracy in America*, trans. from the French by Henry Reese (New York: Alfred A. Knopf, 1945), vol. 1, p. 318.

average and 2 percent believed it poor. In the over-all ranking of the 90 occupations, teachers ranked 36th. U.S. Supreme Court justices ranked first, while shoeshiners came out at the bottom.

In 1963, when the same questions were put to another "cross section" of the American people, teachers had moved up from 36th place to 29.5, in a dead heat with accountants for large business firms. Moreover, during this sixteen-year period, teachers moved ahead of such cultural luminaries as professional artists, novelists, and economists, who now shared a ranking of 34.5.[17] There is some debate, of course, over how much credence one should give this type of sociological pulse-taking. Be that as it may, the status teachers enjoy today is far better than it was in the days when Horace Mann was trying valiantly to bring some order out of the chaos of public education in Massachusetts.

As a group, teachers have more education today. All but 15 percent had the baccalaureate in 1965; those without the degree were mainly older women teachers in the elementary schools.[18] By contrast, in 1920, the percentage of teachers in New York State, outside of New York City, who held college degrees was 11 percent.[19]

Whether or not these added years of formal education have contributed much to the rise in teachers' status and sense of professionalism is another question. The college degree does not have the same distinction it once had. A college degree, Ronald Corwin has pointed out, is less distinctive today than the high-school diploma was in 1900.[20] In educational attainment, teachers have barely kept pace with the rest of the population. Nor does the completion of a college program necessarily mean that the teacher has attained a high degree of intellectual or professional competence, since the training most teachers undergo is still the least rigorous or demanding of any professional program.[21]

Indeed, if one can believe any of the studies that have been made on the intellectual quality of those studying to become teachers, one is

---

[17] Robert E. Hodge, Paul M. Siegel, and Peter H. Rossi, "Occupational Prestige in the United States, 1925–63," *The American Journal of Sociology*, vol. 70, no. 3 (November 1964), pp. 290–292.

[18] National Education Association, *NEA Research Bulletin* (Washington: NEA, 1965), vol. 43, no. 3, p. 69; hereafter referred to by vol. and no.

[19] Homer Cooper, *Cost of Training Teachers* (Baltimore: Warwick and York, 1924), p. 37.

[20] Ronald G. Corwin, "Militant Professionalism, Initiative and Compliance in Public Education," *Sociology of Education*, vol. 38, no. 4 (Summer 1965), p. 312.

[21] For a devastating account of teacher training in America, see James D. Koerner, *The Miseducation of American Teachers* (Boston: Houghton Mifflin Company, 1963).

forced to conclude that most education students might not be able to survive a more rigorous course of study. A recent survey of teacher trainees in New York State, for example, showed that those students who finished the training program and went on to become teachers scored lower on a standard achievement test than non-education majors. The average academic aptitude of teacher trainees, as measured by a test administered by the American Council on Education, was higher only than the group that had flunked out of college.[22] In an earlier study, conducted between the years 1951 and 1953, in which the Selective Service College Qualification Test was administered to almost half a million college men, education majors scored lowest in every year the test was given. While 53 percent of men from all fields — humanities, business, agriculture, science, etc. — scored 70 or higher, only 28 percent of the education majors did as well.[23]

Of course, had similar tests been given in the nineteenth century, the results would have no doubt been even more disappointing. There have been improvements in the intellectual quality of our teachers; admission requirements have been raised in recent years, and a more rigorous curriculum seems to have been introduced in university education schools and in teachers colleges.[24] Yet nineteenth-century attitudes still linger. The public has not yet demanded that those who instruct the young be intellectually superior people.

As we have seen, women first gained a foothold in the teaching profession in the 1840's, and began to dominate the field in the Civil War era. This trend began to be reversed in the late 1940's, however, and by 1965 the percentage of women teachers declined to 65.5 percent[25] from a high of 83 percent forty years earlier. Since the early 1950's, there has been a dramatic increase in the number of men teachers. Between the years 1954 and 1964 the number of men teachers increased by 93 percent, as against a 38 percent increase for women. Men now constitute a majority in the senior high schools and have recently made rather strong inroads into elementary and junior high schools as well.[26]

---

[22] ibid., pp. 44–45.

[23] Educational Testing Service, *Statistical Studies of Selective Service Testing* (Princeton: 1955), p. 40.

[24] One significant development of recent times has been that teachers colleges are being transformed to four-year liberal arts colleges. While most of these continue to be primarily teacher training institutions, the students themselves are being required to major in subject-matter disciplines. As a result there has been a substantial decline in the number of required hours in pedagogy.

[25] *NEA Research Bulletin,* vol. 43, no. 3, p. 68.

[26] ibid., vol. 43, no. 1, p. 8.

For the purpose of this study, this might be the single most important development of recent years. It is also worth pointing out in this context that an increasing proportion of these young men come from blue-collar rather than white-collar backgrounds. In 1957 the proportion was 47 percent.[27] We shall have more to say at a later point on the implications for teacher – school-board relationships of the rising percentage of male teachers. It is sufficient here to suggest that, as a result of this shift in the sex ratio, school boards are faced with changing employee attitudes. Teaching may still be dominated by middle-aged matrons and young women who use the schools as a convenient stopgap between college and marriage, but these groups will no longer set the tone. They are becoming less and less the teachers' spokesmen.

Not only are men coming into teaching in greater numbers, they seem to be staying with it longer, although at first blush the statistics do not appear to bear this out.[28]

Distribution of Classroom Teachers by
Age, Sex, and Experience in Present Systems, 1965–1966.

	Men	Women	All Teachers
Average age	35	41	39.1
Percent under 40 years of age	72.1%	47.3%	56.1%
3 years or fewer teaching experience	41.7%	37.4%	38.9%
4 through 9 years teaching experience	34.8%	28.6%	30.7%
10 years or more teaching experience	23.5%	33.9%	30.6%
Average no. of years teaching experience	6.7	8.6	8.0

But the younger age and shorter experience of men is almost entirely a reflection of their recent entrance into the field, not of a higher rate of

[27] Ward S. Mason, *The Beginning Teacher* (Washington: GPO, 1961), Circular no. 644, p. 13. For professional workers as a whole, only 25 percent had fathers whose occupation was classified as blue-collar.

[28] *NEA Research Bulletin,* vol. 43, no. 3, pp. 69–70.

turnover. Indeed, the turnover rate for teachers seems to have begun to slow down with the entrance of men into teaching in significant numbers. The 8.1 percent loss to the profession in 1960,[29] for example, can probably be attributed more to young women leaving to marry or start families than to young men seeking greener pastures.

William Rabinowitz and Kay Crawford have provided some rather hard evidence on the differences in the teaching persistence of men and women. In their five-year study (1954–1959) of the career patterns of teacher-trainee graduates of various units of the City University of New York, the two researchers found that, while less than half of the women graduates were still teaching in the public schools five years after graduation, over three-fourths of the men were doing so. Equally significant, less than 40 percent of the women teachers planned to continue teaching indefinitely, whereas almost 80 percent of the men saw it as a lifetime career.[30]

What is meant to be suggested by the foregoing is that what was once a mere job has turned into an occupation and is now moving toward a profession. The status of teachers has risen, as has their educational level. In recent years, due partly to the influx of males, teaching has become a more stable enterprise. There have also been, as we shall see, significant increases in salaries and improvements in working conditions.

But this development has not taken place rapidly enough to keep pace with the rising competence and prestige of teachers. The traditions and attitudes of the nineteenth century still hold their grip when it comes to providing teachers with adequate salaries and other benefits.

III

Through the nineteenth century and into the present century, teachers and school boards arrived at salary levels through individual bargaining. The abysmally low salaries teachers received can be attributed at least in part to their lack of bargaining strength vis-à-vis school boards. Also, as one might expect under such an arrangement, there were many opportunities for favoritism. By the second decade of the twentieth century, teachers had become so dissatisfied with this method of setting salaries that they began to press for its abolition.

Whether it was because of teacher pressure or for other reasons,

---

[29] Frank Lindenfeld, *Teacher Turnover in Public, Elementary and Secondary Schools* (Washington: GPO, 1963), Circular no. 675, pp. 7, 17.

[30] William Rabinowitz and Kay E. Crawford, "A Study of Teachers' Careers," *The School Review*, vol. 68, no. 4 (Winter 1960), pp. 385, 387.

individual bargaining began to give way in the middle 1920's to a new system called the "position" schedule. Under this system, salaries were established for each teaching position: first-grade teachers would have one uniform salary, fifth-grade teachers another, and so on. Still another schedule would be established for high-school teachers, almost always higher than that for elementary teachers.

But before the position schedule had been very widely adopted, the "single" or "uniform" salary schedule began to be used in several systems. The practice grew rapidly during the depression and the postwar years. Today it is used in practically all school systems.[31]

Under the single salary schedule, differentials in pay depend solely upon professional preparation and years of teaching experience. When these factors are equal, the kindergarten teacher, the high-school physics teacher, and the driver education teacher all receive the same pay. The following teacher salary schedule covering classroom teachers in Boston, for the 1966–1967 school year, is typical of this type of schedule.[32]

Teachers' Basic Salary Schedule

Step	Bachelor's or Equivalent	Master's	Master's Plus 30	Doctorate
1.	$5,500	$6,000	$6,250	$6,500
2.	5,800	6,300	6,550	6,800
3.	6,100	6,600	6,850	7,100
4.	6,400	6,900	7,150	7,400
5.	6,700	7,200	7,450	7,700
6.	7,000	7,500	7,750	8,000
7.	7,300	7,800	8,050	8,300
8.	7,700	8,200	8,450	8,700
9.	8,100	8,600	8,850	9,100
10.	8,600	9,100	9,350	9,600
11.	9,300	9,800	10,050	10,300

In the immediate postwar period, a number of school districts experimented with what came to be called "merit-pay" schedules. Such

[31] Joseph A. Kershaw and Roland N. McKean, *Teacher Shortages and Salary Schedules* (New York: McGraw-Hill, 1962), pp. 20–23.

[32] *Agreement between the School Committee of the City of Boston and the Boston Teachers' Union* (Classroom teachers and allied personnel), Local 66, Sept. 1, 1966 – Aug. 31, 1967, p. 34.

schedules allowed the administration to pay those teachers who had rendered, in the judgment of the administration, superior service to the school system higher salaries than they would otherwise have received under a normal salary schedule.

Merit-pay plans have not proved to be popular. Teachers complain, to quote a resolution adopted at the 1960 NEA Convention, that "the use of subjective methods [merit ratings] of evaluating professional performance for the purpose of setting salaries has a deleterious effect on the educational process."[33] School officials have readily admitted that such plans are extremely difficult to administer, and neither they nor the teachers seem anxious to see merit systems instituted or continued. Consequently, when in 1960 the NEA polled a sample of those school districts which in the previous twenty years had established provisions for rewarding superior service, it discovered that in 53 percent of the school systems the plans had been abandoned, 20 percent had adopted plans but had not put them into effect, and 18 percent denied that any such plan had ever been adopted. Only 9 percent reported that the plans were still in operation.[34]

Another of the most widely used arguments against merit pay is that it is the wrong way to go about improving the quality of the instructional staff. Only by giving substantial increases across the board, it is often claimed, will the schools be able to attract enough competent college students into teaching. Make teaching competitive with private industry or government service, so the argument runs, and bright, energetic young men and women will apply for teaching jobs in such numbers that no superintendent need ever hire anyone he has doubts about.

Teachers' salaries have increased; average salaries have gone up slightly more than 100 percent between 1950 and 1965, as compared with a 90 percent increase for production workers in industry for the same period.[35] The average salary for classroom teachers during the school

[33] National Education Association of the United States, *Addresses and Proceedings of the Ninety-Eighth Meeting Held in Los Angeles, California, June 26– July 1, 1960*, p. 166.

[34] National Education Association, *Why Have Merit Plans for Teachers' Salaries Been Abandoned?* (Washington: NEA, 1961), Research Report 1961–R3, p. 6. There is some question as to whether or not all of the latter actually have systems of individual awards. Many school officials we have talked to informally indicated that, while there were merit plans in their official school policy, the usual practice had been to give virtually all the teachers the extra increment.

[35] National Education Association, *Economic Status of Teachers in 1963–64* (Washington: NEA, 1964), Research Report 1964–R7, p. 10; *NEA Research Bulletin*, vol. 44, no. 2, p. 36; U. S. Bureau of Labor Statistics, *Employment and Earnings and Monthly Report on the Labor Force* (Washington: GPO, May 1966), vol. 12, no. 11, p. 67.

year 1965–1966 was $6,506. About 9 percent of the 1.7 million public-school employees received less than $4,500; 23 percent received between $4,500 and $5,499; 27 percent from $5,500 to $6,499; 19 percent from $6,500 to $7,499; 12 percent from $7,500 to $8,499; and 10 percent made more than $8,500.[36] It is possible in such places as Bronxville, New York, for a teacher to make as much as $14,275 yearly, but in order to receive that much the teacher must have a doctorate and forty-one years of teaching experience.[37] Probably very few of Bronxville's teachers qualify. Nor are there many places like Bronxville.

It should be noted that attempting to make sense out of average or median salaries is a tricky business. For example, if a school district is expanding rapidly and at the same time has an unusually high turnover rate, teachers could receive a substantial salary increase and at the same time the average salary might remain constant, since new entrants and replacements come in at the bottom of the salary scale. Thus, between the years 1963 and 1965 in the large cities where there had been substantial upward adjustments in salary schedules, the average increase for teachers over the two-year period was only 5.5 percent.[38]

There is no question, however, that teachers' salaries lag far behind those of other professional or paraprofessional workers with similar training. In 1961 the mean annual salary of teachers was $1,000 below that of non-supervisory auditors, $1,500 behind non-supervisory accountants, $1,800 lower than non-supervisory chemists, and $2,700 beneath that of non-supervisory engineers.[39] There seems to have been no substantial change in this ratio in the intervening years.

Nor does there seem to be any prospect for a change in the near future. Entrance salaries for teachers in the fall of 1966 were well below the salary offerings received by other, non-education major, college graduates. Male, bachelor-degree candidates in the humanities and the social sciences, for example, received offers averaging $6,564 yearly; male, bachelor-degree candidates in physics, chemistry, and mathematics

---

[36] *NEA Research Bulletin,* vol. 44, no. 2, p. 36.

[37] National Education Association, *Salary Schedules for Classroom Teachers, 1965–66* (Washington: NEA, 1965), Research Report 1965–R15, p. 120.

[38] "Changes in Teachers Salaries, 1963–65," *Monthly Labor Review,* vol. 88, no. 12 (December 1965), p. 1463.

[39] National Education Association, *The American Public School Teacher, 1960–61* (Washington: NEA, 1963) Research Monograph 1963–M2, p. 20; hereafter referred to by title.

had offers averaging $7,704.[40] The median starting salary for all teachers in September was in the neighborhood of $5,100.[41]

Of course, the last figure includes both men and women (predominantly women) and the others are for men alone. If statistics had been available for both sexes in the non-education category, the gap would have been narrower. Nor does the comparison take into account the qualitative differences between teacher trainees and other college graduates. As was pointed out earlier, since education majors have generally less competence than other college students they would probably command a lower price in the private sector of the labor market. But these omissions do not detract substantially from the main argument, which is that teachers receive significantly smaller salaries than other workers with comparable training and education, that given the present salary arrangements in most school systems it is not likely that many young men and women of real intellectual competence will bother to qualify for a teaching license, and that, as in the nineteenth century, the public today is getting just about as much from its schools as it is willing to pay for.

If this matter of teachers' salaries needs underscoring, recent actions of two official governmental bodies have provided rather interesting emphasis. In 1965 the New York State Legislature fixed minimum teacher salaries at $5,200 for the bachelor's scale, $5,500 for the master's, and $250 as the minimum yearly increment in each scale.[42] A great many school districts, particularly in the upstate area, adopted the state-mandated minimum. In 1966, the same legislative body adopted its controversial "medicaid" program, providing for free medical and dental service to medically needy families. Under the provisions of the law, a breadwinner with three dependents whose net income (after income taxes and health insurance premiums) does not exceed $6,000 and who has modest savings and life insurance coverage is considered medically needy.[43] Thus it is more than theoretically possible that a male teacher with a wife and two children who has a master's degree and has ac-

[40] College Placement Council, *Salary Survey* (Bethlehem, Pa.: College Placement Council, June 1966), p. 7.

[41] National Education Association, *Salary Schedules for Classroom Teachers*, p. 5. This figure is a crude extrapolation of the 1965 starting salary of $5,000.

[42] New York State Education Department, *1965 Summary of New Legislation Affecting Education* (Albany: University of the State of New York, 1965), pp. 17–18.

[43] New York State Department of Social Welfare, *Medical Assistance for Needy Persons* (Albany, N.Y., 1966).

cumulated five years of teaching experience, and who happens to be teaching in one of New York's mandated minimum districts, could be judged medically indigent and eligible for public welfare.

The other case is less significant but equally ironic. In February 1966 when the U.S. Office of Economic Opportunity was requested to fix an hourly rate for the rental of horses in its poverty-fighting program (there was no way other than horseback to reach some of the poverty-stricken in Waldo County, Maine), the Office fixed the rate at $2.00 per hour. A month earlier it had decided that a reasonable rate for elementary school teachers was $2.50 an hour.[44]

One of the reasons Americans have not been very disturbed about low teachers' salaries is that there seems to be a general feeling that, while teachers are not very well paid, they at least have a great many benefits other workers do not have. Such benefits as employer-funded retirement plans, sick leave, health insurance, sabbatic leave, life insurance, and tuition assistance are often cited as examples of "hidden" salary items which, when added to the actual salary, bring teachers up to a par with other professional employees.

It is true that many school districts do provide some or all of these benefits. But as Leslie Wilson has shown in his study of 205 representative school districts during the academic year 1963–1964, it is by no means the case that the dollar value of fringes compensates for the lower salaries. Total fringe benefits accounted for a dollar value of $963 or 13.1 percent of the average professional salary in the systems studied.[45] In private industry during the same year, according to a Bureau of Labor Statistics survey, fringes for other white-collar workers accounted for more than 20 percent of payroll.[46] Nor do most school districts make

---

[44] *Washington Post*, Feb. 28, 1966, p. 1, col. 1.

[45] Leslie Wilson, *The Dollar Value of Fringe Benefits* (New York: Teachers College, Columbia University, 1964), p. 44.

[46] "Report of the Bureau of Labor Statistics to the Joint Economic Committee," February 1966, as quoted in *Daily Labor Report*, Feb. 14, 1966, no. 31, p. B–12.

In another study, done by the Chamber of Commerce (Chamber of Commerce of the United States, *Fringe Benefits,* 1963, Washington: 1964, p. 5), in which a different sample of companies was used and a larger number of items were included in the fringe package, the estimate was 25.6 percent. The difficulty of comparing the dollar amount of fringes for teachers and industry employees is that at times one is comparing apples and oranges. The conditions of employment are radically different. Vacations, for example, are a high-cost fringe item for private employers which do not usually enter into the picture for school boards. Be that as it may, the argument that handsome fringe benefits actually compensate for teachers' low salary levels doesn't hold much water.

14

contributions to all six categories of fringes mentioned earlier, as the table adapted from Wilson's study shows quite clearly.[47]

Hierarchical Order of Relative Importance of Fringe Benefits

	Average Annual District Expenditure per Teacher by District in This Study Which Provide Such Benefits	Percentage of Districts in This Study Which Provide Such Benefits
(1) Retirement (including Social Security)	$822.00	100 %
(2) Sick leave	85.44	100 %
(3) Health insurance	65.60	41.4%
(4) Sabbatical leave	34.48	29.3%
(5) Life insurance	29.01	27.7%
(6) Tuition assistance	13.65	18.7%

A male teacher with family obligations has but three ways to react to the low income his occupation provides. One is to quit teaching, and, as we have seen, many do. Another is to become reconciled to a lower standard of living than other professional groups enjoy, and apparently a great many teachers have accepted this lot. A third way is to take on another job, to "moonlight," and male teachers do this to a greater extent than any other occupational group in our society. In May of 1965, 20 percent of men teachers held second jobs.[48]

For married men with children the percentage was probably much higher. At least that is the indication of a survey of teachers in the Indianapolis area conducted by the Bureau of Economic and Business Research at the University of Illinois in the spring of 1964. For male teachers with children, whose wives worked only part-time, the Bureau found that 38 percent held jobs in addition to teaching and 25 percent

[47] Adapted from Wilson, p. 50.

[48] Forest A. Bogan and Thomas E. Swanstrom, "Multiple Jobholders in May 1965," *Monthly Labor Review*, vol. 89, no. 2 (February 1966), pp. 147, 150.

were self-employed.[49] Even if one allows for considerable duplication, *i.e.* some teachers reporting self-employed *and* employee status, the percentage of moonlighting for teachers in this category would still be above 50 percent. This figure corresponds to the findings of a 1961 NEA survey which reported that 51.5 percent of married male teachers held second jobs during the 1960–1961 school year. The extra job brought them an average of $789 in yearly income.[50]

It would be difficult to say what effect this extra job has on a teacher's classroom performance. A great deal would, of course, depend upon the individual, the nature of the job, and how much time he devotes to it. The NEA is worried about this problem, however, and its revised Code of Ethics, adopted in 1963, reads: "We . . . engage in no outside employment that will impair the effectiveness of our professional service. . . ."[51]

Not all teachers, not even all NEA members, take this admonition seriously. "Who really cares?" a young man wrote to the *NEA Journal* in 1963. "Who cares if the teacher comes in tired the next day? In most schools they rejoice at your mere presence, especially if you are a man. Somehow the administration believes men have magical powers. The only magical power I possess is that of being able to stay awake longer than most people."[52] And when a magazine article reported that two California teachers were running a successful wallpapering and interior decorating business during their off hours, the author received a terse note from the part-time entrepreneurs complaining, "You omitted our names. We [our business] could use the publicity."[53]

IV

If public school teaching does not indeed provide a handsome income, do not teachers have much more job security than most occupations? What about the short hours and the long vacations? And how can one compare salaries and other benefits to the degree of "psychic income" that teachers and other professional workers enjoy?

---

[49] Harold Guthrie, "Who Moonlights and Why," *Illinois Business Review*, vol. 22, no. 3 (March 1965), p. 7.

[50] *The American Public School Teacher, 1960–61*, p. 23.

[51] "Code of Ethics of the Education Profession," *NEA Journal*, vol. 52, no. 4 (April 1963), p. 43.

[52] Sam M. Lambert, "Angry Young Men in Teaching," *NEA Journal*, vol. 52, no. 2 (February 1963), p. 18.

[53] Lambert, "More About the Angry Young Men," *NEA Journal*, vol. 53, no. 5 (May 1963), p. 9.

There is no question about security. Public education is a growing industry with a chronically short labor supply. Schools infrequently cut back in their operations; teachers are rarely laid off. And rarely discharged, one might add. Only 13 percent of those teachers who left school districts for one reason or another at the end of the school year in 1960, for example, were dismissed.[54] How many of these found teaching jobs elsewhere is anybody's guess, but probably more than two-thirds were teaching in another district in a year or two.[55]

All but thirteen of the states, moreover, have tenure laws which protect teachers in their jobs after they have taught from three to four years in a given system. Twenty-six states provide state-wide tenure; in eleven others the laws apply only to certain categories of school districts.[56] And while tenure laws themselves offer wide latitude for discharge even for those who have completed their probationary years (inefficiency, incompetence, immorality, insubordination), the fact that the teacher has the right to appeal to the chief school officer of the state, to the courts, or both makes administrators more cautious than perhaps they should be about firing a teacher who has a tenure appointment. "One of those cases is enough," a superintendent of a large school system remarked to an interviewer in the spring of 1966. "Better to suffer incompetence or even an occasional case of insubordination than put up with a humiliating and demoralizing tenure test case."[57] Thus teachers do indeed have greater job security than most workers; even the dullest among them are protected in their jobs.

On the matter of working conditions, the issue is not so clear-cut. The amount of time teachers are required to be on duty averages about seven and one-half hours daily, including lunch time, which may or may not be duty free. This puts teachers on a 37.5 hour workweek,[58] less than the average for most workers in private employment. Teachers also, of course, have long vacations, more than two months during the summer and from three to four additional weeks during the school year.

Yet, unlike most other occupations, the working day for teachers is by no means limited to time spent at the work place. When teachers were

---

[54] Lindenfeld, p. 5.

[55] Based on the observations of one of the authors who taught for six years in three separate school systems and has seen a great many teachers come and go.

[56] NEA Research Division, *School Law Summaries*, "Tenure and Contracts," November 1964, revised (Washington, D.C.).

[57] Information obtained from a school superintendent, April 28, 1966, in a personal interview.

[58] *NEA Research Bulletin* vol. 43, no. 4, p. 103.

asked in a NEA survey in 1961 to report on actual hours worked, *i.e.* school time plus time spent correcting papers, preparing lessons, working with individual students, and the like, they responded with an average of 47.3 hours.[59] If one takes this estimate at face value and multiplies it by 38, the average number of weeks schools are in session each year,[60] one comes up with an annual rate of slightly less than 1,800 hours, only about 150 hours less than the work year of the employee who works 40 hours a week and has two weeks off for vacation plus five or six paid holidays.

There is no disputing that teaching has rewards one cannot find in other occupations. The psychic income derived from teaching is both a precious and immeasurable commodity. Were it not, the present attrition rate would undoubtedly be much higher than it is. The question is, have events in recent years tended to cause a deterioration in this type of income? One gets the impression that at least in some areas it has. Teachers seem to be complaining more than ever about overcrowded schools which lead to double and triple sessions, large classes, and the growing number of clerical and administrative tasks.[61]

The problem of student discipline, while not a new development, has become considerably exacerbated, particularly in urban schools. On the average of six students a day were arrested for school offenses in Chicago during the early part of 1966, for example, on charges that ranged from loitering to aggravated battery.[62] And when teachers were asked in an NEA poll in 1964 whether they thought it was more difficult to maintain discipline than in previous years, a significant proportion of those with long teaching experience (62 percent of those with 20 or more years)[63] were convinced that it was. Perhaps some of these teachers remembered a past more idealized than real. But this is hardly an adequate explanation. And if teaching has become in many areas what one New

---

[59] *The American Public School Teacher, 1960–61,* p. 103.

[60] *NEA Research Bulletin,* vol. 43, no. 4, p. 103.

[61] For the types of complaints teachers harbor nowadays, see: National Education Association, *What Teachers Think: A Summary of Teacher Opinion Poll Findings, 1960–65* (Washington: NEA, 1965); "What Makes Teachers Burn," *NEA Journal,* vol. 34, no. 5 (May 1966), pp. 13–15; Richard Meryman, "How We Drive Teachers to Quit," *Life,* vol. 30, no. 20 (Nov. 16, 1962), pp. 106–114; National Commission on Teacher Education and Professional Standards, *The Assignment and Misassignment of American Teachers* (Washington: NEA, 1965); on the problem of overcrowding and triple sessions in one urban area, see *New York Times,* April 5, 1966, p. 77, col. 3.

[62] *New York Times,* Feb. 6, 1966, sec. 1, p. 77, col. 3.

[63] National Education Association, *What Teachers Think,* p. 19.

York City teacher has called a "hazardous occupation," then the psychic income can depreciate to the point of deficit.

There are other frustrations, each considerably less dramatic than being confronted with a knife-wielding hoodlum, that nevertheless accumulate to rob teaching of much of its joy and satisfaction. Bel Kaufman has summed up these frustrations in an address delivered before a meeting of the NEA's Commission on Teacher Education and Professional Standards in 1965. The teacher, Miss Kaufman remarked, often finds that "he has no time to teach. He is strangulated by red tape or overwhelmed by clerical work or buried under an avalanche of paper and overwhelmed by five classes, overcrowded homeroom, lunchroom patrol, and lobby duty. He frequently finds that he has no place to teach, and if he is a floater, a peripatetic, unanchored teacher, he is without a room of his own. . . . Teachers are affected by the kind of administration too, with pressures from above and below and the side — administration that frequently does not see the trees for the forest, the young trees and saplings."

"When we get the good teachers and train them well," Miss Kaufman concluded, "then we must give them fewer classes, fewer students, no nonsense to do outside of teaching."[64]

San Francisco's public school teachers sounded a collective Amen to Miss Kaufman's sentiments a few months later. When the San Francisco Classroom Teachers Association, in preparation for negotiations with the local school board, asked its membership to list, in order of priority, those items they wanted the Association to press at the negotiation table, the teachers placed such items as class size, clerical help, and discipline high on the list. As the findings below indicate,[65] salaries were not their greatest concern, although San Francisco is by no means one of the highest paying districts in the nation.

Yet in spite of these mounting frustrations relatively few teachers would choose another occupation if they had it all to do over again. At least that is the way a representative sample felt in 1961 when the NEA asked them about their willingness to teach again if they had the chance to start over. Of the 5,602 respondents to the NEA questionnaire, 49.9 percent said they certainly would and 26.9 percent gave it a strong probability.[66]

---

[64] Bel Kaufman, "Up the Down Staircase," *The Real World of the Beginning Teacher* (Washington: NEA, 1966), pp. 28–30, 33.

[65] *Update* (San Francisco Classroom Teachers Association), vol. 2, no. 2 (February 1966), p. 1.

[66] *The American Public School Teacher, 1960–61,* p. 68.

Top Five Priorities — Items Teachers Wanted Negotiated

Elementary	*Junior High School*	*Senior High School*
1. Class Size	1. Class Size	1. Class Size
2. Discipline	2. Discipline	2. Clerical Help
3. Annual Promotion*	3. Salary	3. Discipline
4. Salary	4. Annual Promotion	4. Salary
5. Clerical Help	5. Clerical Help	5. Fringe Benefits

*Annual promotion has to do with the promotion of students, not teachers.

More interesting for the purposes of this study, however, are those who weren't so sure. Only 34.4 percent of men secondary-school teachers were sure they would do it again as against 60 percent for women elementary-school teachers; 42.8 percent of those from school districts employing 2,500 or more teachers as compared with 55.9 percent in districts that had 1 to 49; 44.7 percent of teachers with the master's degree to 63 percent for teachers with no degree at all; 45.1 percent who had 3 to 9 years teaching experience as against 51.5 percent who had taught less than 3 years and 53.1 percent who had taught more than 20 years.[67] Thus there is a strong probability that a male high-school teacher with a master's degree teaching in an urban area, had he an opportunity to select a new career, would not choose teaching again. And as for the change in attitude that comes about with additional teaching experience — somewhere between his first flush of enthusiasm and the final stage of resignation — lies doubt, resentment, and possibly a sense of entrapment.

V

The current press by teachers to formalize the employment relationship through collective bargaining can be explained in large part by the growing dissatisfaction teachers apparently feel about salaries and working conditions. Salaries, as we have seen, have improved in recent years. But the average teacher still makes about $500 a year less, as a teacher, than the average steelworker,[68] and his income as compared with other occupations, professional and non-professional, seems to have improved hardly at all since Horace Mann's survey of teachers' salaries in Massa-

---

[67] *ibid.*, p. 63.

[68] "Second Test for Early Retirement," *Business Week,* no. 1922, July 2, 1966, p. 75.

chusetts in 1847. And while it is possible for a single woman teacher to buy a new car every third year or so and travel abroad occasionally on the teacher's average yearly income of $6,500, it is not enough for a man to rear his children on, particularly in the style in which he aspires to raise them. We have already commented on the dramatic increase in male teachers.

It would be impossible to document whether teaching conditions have improved or deteriorated over the past several years. Probably student discipline has become more of a problem, at least in urban areas. But in other matters — clerical work, class size, the degree to which teachers are made to perform subprofessional chores — there seems to have been a slight improvement. The point is, however, that teachers today are much more concerned about these problems than before.

There is a certain irony in the fact that, while salaries have increased and working conditions have been somewhat ameliorated, teacher discontent has also increased. Small improvements seem to have aroused the expectation of larger ones. At least it became apparent to some that changes for the better would not come quickly enough or be far-reaching enough if teachers continued to rely solely on the good will of the community and the local school board to bring them about. Such an arrangement denied them effective leverage and left the questions that concerned them the most to unilateral control of school boards and administrators. And concessions which are unilaterally granted, many teachers are beginning to argue, can be unilaterally withdrawn. Consequently, in such school systems as New York City, Detroit, Boston, Rochester, Newark, New Haven, and in hundreds of smaller cities and towns, teachers have begun to bring their collective strength to bear on local school boards. Through bilateral determination, i.e. the collective bargain, they aspire to partnership in establishing the employment arrangement.

But grievances over salaries and working conditions are not the only reasons for this movement toward collective teacher action. Collective bargaining is carried out through organizations. And when there are two national teacher organizations, affiliates of which are vying for members and the right to be the exclusive representatives of teachers before their employers, this competition can in itself stimulate interest and activity. The rivalry between the National Education Association and the American Federation of Teachers, as we shall see in the next chapter, is almost as important a cause of the present efforts to formalize the employer-employee relationship in public education as is dissatisfaction with conditions of work.

II

The Public School Teacher
as Organization Man

IT IS RARE THAT TWO ORGANIZATIONS markedly dissimilar in origin, structure, and style should come to pursue identical objectives in similar fashion. Yet as one looks at recent activities of affiliates of the National Education Association and the American Federation of Teachers, organizations which over the years have held widely differing views on the proper role of teacher associations, one is impressed more by similarities than by differences. The catalyst has been the movement to formalize the employment relationship in public schools, and the organization that has done most of the reacting has been the NEA. The circumstances created by collective bargaining have forced a great many NEA affiliates to adopt functions and even an outlook more typical of trade unions than of professional organizations. The AFT has veered less from its appointed course. One sees in the AFT's current interest in problems of education distinct from the employment relationship, however, a somewhat determined effort to achieve professional respectability.

But while it is true that the two teacher organizations are beginning to show a strong resemblance to one another, many differences remain. And one can probably get a better understanding of the current movement among teachers to formalize the employment relationship by briefly exploring these differences.

One of the most obvious differences is in longevity. The NEA was founded in 1857, as the National Teachers Association, when representatives of ten state teacher associations gathered to form a national organization they hoped would "elevate the character and advance the interests of the profession of teaching, and ... promote the cause of popular education in the United States."[1] Reflecting the masculine domination of the profession of that era, the new association limited its membership to "gentlemen."

The first sixty years of the NEA did not prove to be very promising. Although membership rose to over 9,000 in 1887, it fell to little more than a thousand in the late 1890's and did not achieve 10,000 until 1918, when it enrolled about 5 percent of American public school teachers.[2] Only five departments — school administration, vocational education, science education, business education, and kindergarten education — were created in the nineteenth century, and it was not until 1914 that the Classroom Teachers Association, today the largest of the NEA departments, was organized.[3]

By 1966, however, membership totaled about 900,000, with an additional 600,000 teachers and administrators affiliated with state associations. The number of departments, divisions, and commissions had risen to seventy-four, providing services to such diverse groups as social science and mathematics teachers, elementary teachers, school administrators, curriculum specialists, teacher-training institutions, and parent-teacher associations.

The AFT was organized in Chicago in 1916 when the Chicago Teachers Federation, which had been in existence since 1897, joined with the Chicago Federation of Women Teachers, the Chicago Federation of Men Teachers, and a teachers' local in Gary, Indiana, to secure a charter as an affiliate of the American Federation of Labor.[4] From the beginning, the AFT seems to have concentrated on conditions of employment. The two primary objectives stated in its constitution were to "obtain for [teachers] all the rights to which they are entitled," and "to raise the standards of the teaching profession by securing the conditions essential to the best professional service."[5] The way to "elevate the character of the profession of teaching," evidently, was to put the stress on teachers' freedom and economic well-being. And there was a lesson to be learned from unionized craft workers of that era who, because they bargained collectively with their employers, seemed to enjoy more on-the-

---

[1] Edgar B. Wesley, *The NEA: The First Hundred Years* (New York: Harper and Brothers, 1957), pp. 23–24. The organization changed its name to National Education Association in 1870.

[2] *ibid.*, p. 397.

[3] *ibid.*, pp. 278–281.

[4] The Commission on Educational Reconstruction, *Organizing the Teaching Profession* (Glencoe, Ill.: The Free Press, 1955), pp. 27–28.

[5] *ibid.*, p. 28.

job freedom and economic well-being than did teachers. Although collective bargaining did not become an immediate objective of AFT affiliates, it eventually became the most distinguishing feature separating the union from the NEA.

Like the NEA, the AFT had difficulty getting off the ground. Twenty years after it was founded, it had only 13,000 members. But it doubled its membership during the depression (while the NEA was losing members) and took another spurt between 1962 and 1966 when membership rose from 60,000 to over 120,000,[6] making it one of the fastest growing trade unions of modern times.

The AFT is still very largely an employee organization. True, it has recently expanded its research efforts and in 1966 launched a new "professional" journal, *Changing Education,* and a series of pamphlets in its Grassroots Research Project dealing with problems in education. It has also developed an interest in teacher training and recruitment, and in its More Effective Schools program has been instrumental in bringing about some imaginative innovations in staffing and educational practices in slum schools in a handful of cities. But for the most part AFT activities have been self-serving with some activities being carried out, it would appear, only in an attempt to "one-up" the NEA.

Since the NEA is essentially a professional association and the AFT primarily an employee organization, there are, as one might expect, significant structural differences. Membership in the NEA, for example, is direct, teachers usually having the option of joining the national, state, or local organizations (or all three) on an individual basis. State and local affiliates are only loosely tied in with the national association.

The AFT is organized along more typical trade union lines. Teachers join an AFT local, which usually claims jurisdiction over an entire school district or system, and the local in turn pays a per capita tax to the national organization. In those states where there is a state federation, it too derives its funds from a per capita tax on the locals.

The real strength of the NEA is in its state affiliates. More than half again as many teachers are members of the state associations as of the national. In New York State, for example, NEA membership is about

[6] American Federation of Teachers, *Representing Today's Teachers* (Chicago: AFT, 1964), p. 69; *American Teacher,* May 1966, p. 1, col. 1.

one-third that of the New York State Teachers Association.[7] The reason for this, beyond the fact that state associations existed long before the NEA was organized, is that public education, in the final analysis, is a function of the states. It is the state legislature, NEA spokesmen point out, that establishes teacher tenure laws, retirement and welfare plans, and minimum (which often turn out to be maximum) salaries. State governments also provide a large percent of school revenue, over 40 percent on the average, to local school districts. Thus, it is argued, if one truly wishes to represent the interests of teachers one must organize to deal with those who make the most significant decisions affecting teacher welfare — the state legislature and education department.

The AFT, on the other hand, while certainly not ignoring developments in state capitals, has put most of its eggs in the local school district basket. The state legislature might have an important hand in determining the size of total educational appropriations, but it is usually the local school board, union members point out, that determines how this money shall be spent. Furthermore, if AFT affiliates are to bargain over conditions of employment, they must strike the bargain with local authorities who, as distinct from state officials, have sufficient discretion to make adjustments in the employment arrangement in the here and now. The strike, or threat thereof, has become the most potent union weapon for gaining concessions.

State and local associations have, until recently, relied almost exclusively on sanctions for the same purpose. Teachers are warned that employment conditions in a given state or locality are unsatisfactory, and those employed in the areas under sanctions are assisted in finding employment elsewhere. The publicity accompanying a vote of sanctions, moreover, can have a chilling effect on governors, legislatures, and local school boards and administrators. The NEA's use of sanctions is partly due to its aversion to the strike but, equally important, because it is a measure that is consistent with its unique structure. If one wants to apply pressure on a state governor or legislature, as state associations

---

[7] *NEA Reporter,* June 17, 1966, p. 2, col. 1. NEA membership seems to be concentrated in the West. As of 1966 only California and Colorado of all Rocky Mountain and Pacific Coast states had less than 75 percent of all school employees enrolled in the NEA. By contrast, Louisiana had 11 percent and Rhode Island 12 percent. Of the large cities, New York, where the United Federation of Teachers, an affiliate of the AFT, has represented all teachers since 1962, has the lowest percentage — 3 percent. AFT strength, as of 1965, was concentrated in Rhode Island, where 26.9 percent of all teachers were members; New York, 22.8 percent; Illinois, 20.0 percent; Minnesota, 16.3 percent; Michigan, 14.5 percent.

have done in Utah, Kentucky, and Oklahoma in recent years, then the pressure must be state-wide. If the problem is at the local district level and the local association is weak, as most of them are, then only the state and the national association can muster the necessary leverage, via sanctions, to win concessions from the school board.

Another significant difference between the two organizations is in the composition of the local affiliates. NEA groups, in keeping with the national organization's principle of community of interest between teachers and administrators, typically seek to recruit all certificated school personnel as members. Thus in 1966 school superintendents were eligible for membership in almost 75 percent of local teachers' associations. Only 12.4 percent of local associations confined membership to classroom teachers.[8]

AFT affiliates are more inclined, as are most trade unions, to restrict membership to non-supervisory personnel. Only 17.6 percent allow principals as members, according to a 1966 survey of 262 locals comprising about 70 percent of AFT membership, and 19.5 percent admit assistant principals. Department heads in junior and senior high schools are eligible for membership in 58 percent of AFT locals, however.[9]

The significance of the composition of the two rival organizations lies in the influence this composition has on determining the bargaining unit when teachers begin to press for formalization of the employment relationship in a local district. Ideology aside, the group that has the largest number of members voting in a representation election has a better chance of being selected as the exclusive bargaining agent. Thus one finds NEA affiliates very often demanding all-inclusive units, since they have considerable membership among administrative personnel, and AFT groups plugging for units consisting of classroom teachers only where *their* strength is concentrated.

The AFT's position on limiting the bargaining unit to non-supervisory personnel has had an unexpected advantage, however. The NEA is associated in teachers' eyes with the educational establishment, and teachers who feel aggrieved by the conditions of their employment often blame the establishment for their predicament, or at the very least accuse it of not doing enough to improve their circumstances. The NEA and its state and local affiliates have long been *the* organizations in

---

[8] Information in a letter to the authors from Glen Robinson, director, Research Division, NEA, August 23, 1966.

[9] Pete Schnaufer, *Report on Supervisory Membership in the AFT and in Other International Unions*, A Report Prepared for the Executive Council of the American Federation of Teachers, 1966, p. 1.

public education, and to many teachers they just have not delivered the goods. To support the Association in a representation election then would be tantamount to giving one's approval of doing the same old business at the same old stand. Thus, in Philadelphia, the local AFT affiliate went into a representation election in 1965 with slightly more than 2,000 members against the Association's 5,200, yet won the election handily.[10]

Another advantage enjoyed by the AFT is that the NEA has long had a reputation of using subtle, and sometimes not so subtle, administrative pressure to get teachers to join the organization. Probably there has been a marked decline over the last several years in the number of school districts where Association membership is, for all practical purposes, compulsory. But teacher resentment lingers, and the privacy afforded by the secret ballot in a representation election provides an excellent opportunity to show it.

If the AFT has accomplished anything, it has exposed the efforts of school administrators to force Association membership on reluctant teachers. Yet compulsion does remain in some quarters. As recently as 1965, the California Senate Fact-finding Committee on Governmental Administration reported that "the right of certificated public school employees to 'join' . . . or 'refuse to join' . . . employee organizations of their own choosing," a right guaranteed under California law, "is being interfered with, abridged, and violated on a widespread basis. . . ."[11] The report continued that legal remedies available to provide redress did not provide practical relief, that ratings, promotions, and recommendations for tenure were very often dependent on membership in the California Teachers Association, that subtle oral pressure was as influential as official written policy, and that such pressure is bound to continue so long as administrators, who do the rating and make the recommendations, are also members of the Association.[12] California might be an extreme case, but it is not easy to understand how the Teachers Association of the State of Washington could boast of a 100 percent membership in 1966[13] without assuming overzealousness on the part of local school administrators anxious to fill their membership quotas.

Of course, the NEA aspires to be a professional association, the func-

[10] *White Collar Report,* no. 413, Feb. 4, 1965, p. A-4.

[11] *Final Report on Compulsory Membership in Professional Organizations Among Credentialed California School Employees.* Senate of the State of California, 1965, p. 16.

[12] *ibid.*

[13] *NEA Reporter,* June 17, 1966, p. 2, col. 1.

tion of which is to enhance the status of education, rather than to serve merely as an employee organization. And it should be pointed out that the high percentage of teachers and administrators in state associations, about 84 percent on a national average, is about on a par with the degree of professional affiliation of the two most respected professions, medicine and law.

An interesting sidelight on the NEA's competition with the AFT is that one of its most important professional tenets — the obligation to police its own ranks — seems to be eroding away. As a professional organization, the NEA has felt over the years that it should be as much concerned about the professional conduct and teaching competence of its members as about their economic welfare. One gets the impression, in reading the literature of the Committee on Professional Ethics and the Commission on Professional Rights and Responsibilities over the past years, that the NEA and its affiliates were to be judges as well as advocates, that responsibilities of teachers were to be given at least as much importance as their rights. By 1966, however, with the pressure to win representation elections and the duty to represent teachers, a duty that collective bargaining imposes in a rather special way, there seems to have been a sloughing off of the obligation to judge, and teachers' rights appear to be stressed more vigorously than their obligations. The lesson, evidently, is that if one competes with a union, one ends up playing by the union's rules.

Superficially viewed, there are no significant differences between the rank-and-file members of the two organizations, except that, as William Lowe has pointed out, the AFT has a much higher percentage of males than does the NEA and the profession generally.[14] The AFT also has a higher percentage of junior and senior high-school teachers, but that is where the men are. Also, as Professor Lowe has indicated, AFT members are more inclined to be members of professional bodies such as the National Council for the Teaching of Social Studies or the National Science Teachers Association, both organizations, incidentally, organs of the NEA. But, here again, these are associations that cater to subject-matter specialists who are almost always on the junior and senior high-school level, a high percentage of whom, over half, are men. As to other characteristics, dissatisfaction with teaching as a career, the degree to which they feel intimidated by administrators, professional competence,

---

[14] William T. Lowe, "Who Joins Which Teachers Group?" *Teachers College Record*, vol. 66, no. 7 (April 1965), pp. 615–616.

interest in the welfare of school children, there seem to be no significant differences.[15]

There is a rather striking difference in the matter of style, however. While the NEA has a record of solid accomplishments in the professional area, it is also, paradoxically, plagued by a reputation for complacency in the face of real educational problems. There is little sense of urgency in its manner, not much tough-minded intellectualism in its posture. The 1965 NEA Convention in New York City, wrote Fred Hechinger, was "a mixture of conventioneering corn and prissy schoolmarmism . . . an embarrassing kind of image building, in conflict with the aims of action-minded and intellectually oriented delegates. . . . Embarrassingly little discussion of educational substance, philosophy, issues of research came from within the public school ranks."[16]

But if the NEA often seems prissy and complacent, the AFT sometimes gives the impression of stridency — its criticisms of school boards, administrators, the "establishment" being characterized more by their shrillness than by their telling accuracy. The AFT has opted for, and appears to relish, the role of the abused underdog, clashing valiantly with school boards and the competing Association. One finds in its literature, the monthly *American Teacher,* in its occasional publications, even in its new professional quarterly, *Changing Education* (the front cover of the first issue carried an Osborn cartoon showing a supervisor sitting on top of the head of a bound and gagged teacher), a sense of victimization that almost borders on the paranoiac. Brave and dedicated Federation members, evidently, are daily being exploited by cruel and reactionary administrations.

Two recent actions by the AFT, both prompted by its affiliation with the AFL-CIO, and the subsequent reaction of the NEA, serve as excellent examples of stylistic differences between the two organizations. One had to do with the AFT's support of a strike by five unions against the Kingsport Press in Kingsport, Tennessee, one of the nation's largest manufacturers of school textbooks. The background of the dispute, briefly, is that the unions struck against Kingsport in 1963 for higher wages and other benefits, but the company kept operating with the help of supervisors, workers who had abandoned the strike, and "permanent"

---

[15] *ibid.,* pp. 617–618; Lesley Hughes Browder, Jr., "Teacher Unionism in America: A Descriptive Analysis," Ph.D. Dissertation, School of Education, Cornell University, 1965, pp. 194–226.

[16] Fred Hechinger, "NEA Convention Rich in Hoopla," *New York Times,* July 4, 1965, sec. 4, p. 5, col. 2.

replacements. By the spring of 1966, over 1,000 of the original 1,600 strikers were still out.[17]

At its 1965 Convention, the AFT adopted a resolution supporting the strikers and urging member locals "to call on their local boards of education to refrain from purchasing books printed by the Kingsport Press."[18] By 1966, two big city school boards, New York City and Cleveland, had been persuaded by the AFT and other unions, mostly in the printing trades, to boycott Kingsport Press books if, in the judgment of building principals, other books of "equal value" were available. The unions argued that taxpayers' money should not be used to support firms paying substandard wages.

"The AFT demonstrated, beyond a shadow of a doubt, where its first loyalties lay," the NEA *Urban Reporter* charged in the fall of 1965. "Given a choice between the principles of academic freedom for teachers and youth's right to learn vs. paying off its debts to other labor unions on whose financial and manpower support it is so completely dependent, the AFT chose the latter.[19] . . . Clearly, the price of unionism is costly for teachers. They are, in effect, being asked to forfeit professional judgment and responsibility and leave educational decisions to non-professionals who are motivated by responsibilities and interests which are, and must remain, extraneous to the teaching-learning process."[20]

The NEA position was that professionally trained teachers should be intimately involved in the selection of textbooks and other teaching materials. And while the Association held no brief for the uncompromising stand of the employer in the Kingsport dispute, it maintained that the dispute itself should not be allowed to intrude into the schools. The consequence of a school board boycott would be to make teachers "voiceless bystanders, indifferent to questions of educational excellence,"[21] a circumstance that is in rather sharp contrast to the role both the AFT and the NEA would like teachers to play.

The other issue on which the two organizations are divided is support of the sales tax as a source of school revenue. Because of their affiliation with state and local AFL-CIO bodies, which oppose this form of taxa-

---

[17] *New York Times,* Feb. 13, 1966, p. 65, col. 2.

[18] American Federation of Teachers, AFL-CIO, *Proceedings of the Forty-ninth Annual Convention, Los Angeles, California, August 23-27, 1965,* p. 115.

[19] "AFT'S 'Ban-the-Books' Caper Imperils Academic Freedom," *Urban Reporter,* vol. 4, no. 3 (November 1965), p. 1.

[20] *ibid.,* p. 6.

[21] "New York City Board Votes to Ban-the-Books," *Urban Reporter,* vol. 4, no. 6 (April-May 1966), p. 1.

tion, AFT locals have fought against passage of sales-tax laws or increases in several states, counties, and municipalities.[22] The argument against the sales tax, of course, is that such taxes are regressive. They place the burden on low-income families which spend a higher *proportion* of their income on consumer goods than the well-to-do and therefore have to pay a disproportionate percentage of the tax.

The counterargument, originally advanced by John Kenneth Galbraith, but picked up by the NEA and its state and local affiliates, is that unlike other forms of taxation — property, income, excise — the yield of the sales tax responds immediately to increases in the production of consumer goods. And as wants increase for consumer goods more revenue is created for public use. As Galbraith has put it, "... by making private goods more expensive, public goods are made more abundant. Motion pictures, electronic entertainment, and cigarettes are made more costly so that schools can be more handsomely supported."[23]

The sales-tax issue has put many AFT locals in a difficult position. They are allied, or at least closely identified, with organizations that oppose the tax, even though much, sometimes all, of the revenue is earmarked for support of public education. AFT locals in Oklahoma and Louisiana evidently lost a great deal of momentum in their organizing drives when the state labor bodies came out against sales-tax increases.[24]

Like the textbook boycott, the AFT's position on the sales-tax issue will probably prove to be a source of embarrassment to its members. Certainly it will not help the union in its organizing drives. Nor is the AFT's stand on the textbook ban calculated to endear it to the intellectual community.

II

In the previous chapter we pointed out some of the reasons many teachers are demanding some type of formalized employment arrangement with local school boards. The dramatic increase in the number of

---

[22] "New Jersey School Support Battle Pits the NJEA Against the AFL-CIO," *Urban Reporter,* vol. 4, no. 6 (March-April 1966), p. 8; "AFL-CIO Opposition Fails to Defeat Baton Rouge Sales Tax for Schools," *Urban Reporter,* vol. 4, no. 5 (January-February 1966), p. 6; Barbara Cater, "The Teachers Give Oklahoma a Lesson," *The Reporter,* vol. 33, no. 4 (Sept. 9, 1965), p. 35.

[23] John Kenneth Galbraith, *The Affluent Society* (Boston: Houghton Mifflin Company, 1958), p. 315.

[24] Cater, p. 35; "AFL-CIO Opposition Fails to Defeat Baton Rouge Sales Tax for Schools," p. 6.

men teachers, low salaries, unsatisfactory working conditions, the mounting frustrations of public school teaching headed the list.

But there is another reason — the growing competition between the two major teacher organizations — that might be as important a cause of organizational activity as all the other reasons combined. This competition has its roots in the changing character of the work force and the frustrations it presents to the labor movement. "Feeling the effects of declining employment and membership in manufacturing and other traditional areas of union strength," Ronald Donovan has observed, ". . . and generally concerned about a decline in strength and influence, the labor movement sees the governmental sector as a promising field."[25]

Public employment is indeed a beckoning frontier for a stagnated labor movement. Employment in state and local government rose by 74 percent between 1951 and 1964, when it reached a total of 7.16 million[26] with only about 1.5 million represented by trade unions.[27] At the same time, there has been a significant increase in white-collar employment, 27.7 percent from 1950 to 1960; yet as of 1964 only about 11 percent of white-collar workers were organized.[28] This area too, in Professor Donovan's expression, is a promising field for organized labor to harvest.

Teachers, being both public employees and white-collar workers, posed a fat target for unionization. Salaries were low; there were numerous complaints about working conditions; the major teacher organization appeared to be indifferent to the employment arrangement, or at least unable to make improvements in it; and there was already a union of teachers, albeit small and ineffective, which had been affiliated with the American labor movement for a good many years. It was also thought that, if teachers could become organized and receive substantial benefits thereby, this might serve as an inducement to other government and white-collar workers to join up.

Thus, when the United Federation of Teachers in New York City, an AFT affiliate, led a successful strike in 1962 that culminated in the first comprehensive collective agreement covering teachers, the labor movement was encouraged that this might be just the "breakthrough" it was waiting for. So it was viewed at least by the AFL-CIO's Industrial

[25] Ronald Donovan, "Labor Relations in the Public Service," *Industrial and Labor Relations Report Card,* vol. 14, no. 3 (March 1966), p. 3.

[26] *ibid.,* p. 1.

[27] *ibid.,* p. 3.

[28] Everett M. Kassalow, "White-Collar Unionism in the United States," *White-Collar Trade Unions: Contemporary Developments in Industrialized Societies,* Adolf Sturmthal, ed. (Urbana: University of Illinois Press, 1966), pp. 307, 338.

Union Department, a collection of former CIO and other industrial unions which for some time had been spearheading the drive to organize white-collar and government employees. Money was poured into AFT organizing drives and representation elections, $362,000 between 1963 and 1965,[29] highly skilled manpower was donated to assist AFT locals in election contests, and in 1965 prestige was added to money and manpower when AFT president Charles Cogen was made an IUD vice-president. With IUD help, the AFT went on to win representation elections in Detroit, Cleveland, Philadelphia, Boston, Yonkers, and dozens of smaller school systems.

To the NEA, what had been merely an irritant had now become a major threat. It could either play the union's game, the two chief rules of which were exclusive recognition and collective bargaining, or face the possibility of being eased out as a viable organization in urban and suburban communities. It chose to play, sometimes by demanding representation elections before the union could muster sufficient strength, as in Rochester, New York, but in other cases responding successfully to union-initiated requests, as in Newark, New Jersey. Once elected as the exclusive bargaining agent, the Association had no choice but to negotiate comprehensive, very "union-like" agreements. This was particularly the case in those instances where the union was in the wings, waiting for the Association to fall on its face — Newark, New Haven, New Rochelle.

In the process, several local associations became transformed. Salary requests came to be called salary demands, consultation was changed to negotiation, professional associations began to look and sound like employee organizations. Teachers who had never dreamed of bilateral determination of employment conditions now talked in the jargon of trade unionism, and school administrators and school boards who had once been thought of as captains of the team were now in a few instances being regarded as exploiters. To be sure, competition between the two organizations had its origin in unsatisfactory employment arrangements, but by 1966 this competition seemed to be its own *raison d'être*. Issues were raised as much for the way in which they served the institutional interests of competitors as for their merit. Collective bargaining which emerged as a consequence of teacher unrest was, because of the intensity of the AFT-NEA rivalry, proving in some cases to be its cause.

The emergence of a viable AFT has also been responsible for a rather significant transformation of the NEA at the national level. The attitude of the NEA toward bilateral determination of working conditions,

---

[29] *Government Employee Relations Reporter,* no. 115, Nov. 22, 1965, p. B-1.

at least as reflected by its Delegate Assembly, has since 1960 undergone a rather profound change. Thus in 1960 when a rather innocuous resolution on the "representative Conference," a term used by the NEA at that time as a euphemism for professional negotiations, was brought to the convention for adoption it was considered a bit too rich for the blood of most delegates and was sent to the NEA Board of Directors for further consideration.[30] The following year a similar resolution, saying that professional associations "*should* be accorded the right . . . to participate in the determination of policies of common concern including salary and other conditions for professional service"[31] passed the convention by an overwhelming majority.

Not until 1962, however, did the Delegate Assembly really get down to the business of spelling out what this new process, now called professional negotiations, actually meant. The fact that the UFT had negotiated a comprehensive agreement that spring, and that the AFT had picked up almost 10,000 members between 1960 and 1962 undoubtedly caused some consternation among NEA leaders. The 1962 resolution, which is regarded by the Association as a new departure in its thinking on how school boards should be dealt with, is reproduced below in full.

> The teaching profession has the ultimate aim of providing the best possible education for all the people. It is a professional calling and a public trust. Boards of education have the same aims and share this trust.
> *The National Education Association calls upon boards of education in all school districts to recognize their identity of interest with the teaching profession.*
> The National Education Association *insists* on the right of professional associations, through democratically selected representatives using professional channels, to participate with boards of education in the determination of policies of common concern, including salary and other conditions of professional service.
> Recognizing both the legal authority of boards of education and the educational competencies of the teaching profession, the two groups should view the consideration of matters of mutual concern as a joint responsibility.
> The seeking of consensus and mutual agreement on a professional basis should preclude the arbitrary exercise of unilateral authority of boards of education and *the use of the strike by teachers.*

---

[30] National Education Association, *Addresses and Proceedings of the Ninety-eighth Annual Meeting, Los Angeles, California, June 26–July 1, 1960*, p. 160.

[31] National Education Association, *Addresses and Proceedings of the Ninety-ninth Annual Meeting, Atlantic City, N.J., June 25–30, 1961*, pp. 216–217 (italics added).

The Association believes that procedures should be established which provide an orderly method for professional education associations and boards of education to reach mutually satisfactory agreements. These procedures should include provisions for appeal through designated educational channels when agreement cannot be reached.

Under no circumstances should the resolution of differences between professional associations and boards of education be sought through channels set up for handling industrial disputes. The teacher's situation is completely unlike that of an industrial employee. A board of education is not a private employer, and a teacher is not a private employee. Both are committed to serve the common indivisible interest of all persons and groups in the community in the best possible education for their children. Teachers and boards of education can perform their indispensible functions only if they act in terms of their identity of purpose in carrying out this commitment. Industrial-disputes conciliation machinery, which assumes a conflict of interest and a diversity of purpose between persons and groups, is not appropriate to professional negotiations in public education.

The National Education Association calls upon its members and upon boards of education to seek state legislation and local board action which clearly and firmly establishes these rights for the teaching profession.[32]

The resolution adopted in 1963 was essentially the same as the 1962 resolution. But in 1964 the delegates voted to drop the caveat about local associations using "channels set up for handling industrial disputes" and added a section commending school boards, superintendents, and associations that had already "initiated and entered into written negotiation agreements."[33] The following year the phrase condemning "the use of the strike by teachers" was omitted, and while the 1965 resolution did not go so far as to say that there was an inherent conflict between teachers and school boards, it did for the first time "recognize[s] that the school board, the superintendent or administration, and the teaching staff have significantly different contributions to make in the development of educational policies and procedures."[34] Truly, a lot had happened since 1960.

---

[32] National Education Association, *Addresses and Proceedings of the One-Hundredth Annual Meeting, Denver, Colorado, July 1–July 6, 1962*, p. 397 (italics added).

[33] National Education Association, *Addresses and Proceedings of the One-Hundred-and-Second Annual Meeting, Seattle, Washington, June 28–July 3, 1964*, p. 446.

[34] National Education Association, *Addresses and Proceedings of the One-Hundredth Annual Meeting, Denver, Colorado, July 1–July 6, 1962*, p. 397 (italics added).

It was probably in connection with this new mood that the delegates acted during the 1965 Convention to drain much of the substance from the charge that the NEA was administrator-dominated and, therefore, little more than a "company union." If local affiliates were to compete successfully with the AFT, the NEA would have to persuade classroom teachers that the parent organization was not only for them but of them as well. "At present our opponents' contention is that the NEA is moving too slowly to give vital assistance to classroom teachers in this country,"[35] one delegate complained. And if there was a ring of truth in this contention it might have been, as Thelma Davis, president of the Classroom Teachers Department, pointed out, because: "Since the year 1947 up to 1964 we have had no representation on the Board of Trustees . . . [and] since 1950 no members who were classroom teachers have been elected by the Board of Directors to serve on the Executive Committee."[36]

The teacher delegates voted overwhelmingly to rectify the matter. The NEA bylaws were changed so that at least one of the two members elected by the Board of Directors to the Executive Committee would be a classroom teacher, as would at least two of the four members elected by the convention. The change also provided that at least two members of the Board of Trustees elected by the Board of Directors should be classroom teachers. The amendments passed by votes of 4,669 to 1,298 and 4,472 to 1,366, respectively.[37]

Other developments within the Association also pointed to a changing attitude toward the manner in which teachers should participate in the formulation of school policies affecting the employment arrangement. The Office of Urban Services, in effect the NEA's collective bargaining arm, although not established until 1962, had by 1965 a budget that accounted for 13 percent of all NEA expenditures.[38] It is also instructive to look at the changes that have taken place in the various revisions of the NEA booklet, *Professional Negotiations: Selected Statements of School Board, Administrator, Teacher Relationships.* First published in 1963, the booklet was designed as a guide for local associations contemplating a more formalized relationship with their school boards. In both the 1963 edition and the 1964 revision, the majority of examples of professional agreements cited were of the Level I and Level II variety, providing only for "recognition" and "recognition plus outline of nego-

---

[35] *ibid.,* p. 120.
[36] *ibid.,* p. 122.
[37] *ibid.,* p. 223
[38] *ibid.,* p. 379.

tiation procedure," respectively. In the 1965 revision, however, there was but one example each of the Level I and II categories. The remaining space was devoted to excerpts from Level III agreements, which are very much like the comprehensive labor-management contracts used in private employment. We shall have more to say about the nature of these agreements later; it need only be said here that by 1965 the NEA had evidently come around to accepting the same type of elaborate document the AFT had long been advocating.

If NEA affiliates are less inclined to strike than union locals, there nonetheless appears to be declining aversion to work stoppages among NEA members. The local Association in Newark did go out in the spring of 1966 when it reached an impasse with the board over salaries, and in the same year in Michigan four NEA affiliates were out on strike at the same time. Elsewhere there have been strike threats and threats of mass resignation when local boards were slow in granting minimum concessions. The deletion of the stricture on strikes from the NEA resolution on professional negotiations in 1965 might have been in anticipation of this kind of militancy. The delegates might also have been anticipating the results of an NEA survey under way at that time. For when the Association asked a national teacher sample in late 1965 and early 1966 if teachers should ever strike, it found that, while only 3.3 percent thought teachers should have the same strike rights as any other group of employees, 50 percent believed strikes were permissible under extreme circumstances. Sixty-one percent of this group thought low salaries an extreme circumstance. Not surprisingly, male teachers and teachers in large school districts opposed strikes to a markedly lesser degree than women or those from small districts.[39]

And when the NEA Convention dropped its opposition to using "industrial channels" for establishing election procedures and dispute-settlement machinery, the reason might have been that, in those states where laws covering employee relations in public service forced affiliates to operate under the industrial model (Wisconsin and Michigan), local associations were doing very well indeed. As of the spring of 1966, Michigan NEA affiliates had won 48 of the 68 representation elections conducted under the public employee bargaining statute, and represented 51,900 teachers, as against the union's 15,770, including 10,500 in Detroit. The Association's record was even better in Wisconsin, where it had won 18 of 23 elections and had been designated as exclusive

---

[39] "Teacher Opinion Poll: Should Teachers Strike?" *NEA Journal*, vol. 55, no. 5 (May 1966), p. 54.

representative through stipulations in 100 more.[40] And while they might have found it upsetting, it probably came as no surprise to members of the Wisconsin School Boards Association when the Wisconsin Education Association passed a resolution at its annual meeting late in 1965 stating: "The Wisconsin Education Association *opposes* action which seeks to nullify or amend Statute 11.70 [providing for collective bargaining for municipal and county employees] in such ways as to exclude teachers from enjoying the benefits, rights and prerogatives listed therein."[41]

III

The quintessence of the formalized employment arrangement is the collective agreement, or contract, which sets forth in detail those employment conditions that have been bilaterally determined. There is no better way to compare the ultimate objectives of AFT and NEA affiliates, at least as far as employer-employee relations are concerned, than to examine the contents of the agreements that have been negotiated by both organizations.[42]

---

[40] *Government Employee Relations Reporter,* no. 140, May 16, 1966, p. B-5. The Massachusetts statute covering bargaining rights for public employees did not go into effect until February of 1966, too short a time before this was written to permit an assessment of how well the Association was doing.

[41] Quoted in an address by George E. Watson to the Joint School Board-Administrator Convention, Milwaukee, Jan. 21, 1966 (italics added).

[42] The agreements alluded to here and throughout this section are: *Agreement between the Board of Education of the City of Detroit and the Detroit Federation of Teachers, Local 231, AFT,* June 29, 1965–July 1, 1966; *Agreement between the Grosse Pointe Board of Education and the Grosse Pointe Education Association,* July 1, 1966–June 30, 1970; *Agreement between the Highland Park Board of Education and Highland Park Federation of Teachers,* July 1, 1966–July 1, 1967; *Agreement between the New Haven Board of Education and the New Haven Teachers' League* (affiliated with the NEA), January 17, 1966–January 16, 1969; *Agreement between the New Rochelle Teachers Association and the Board of Education of the City School District of New Rochelle,* July 1, 1964–June 30, 1965; *Agreement between the Board of Education of the City School District of New Rochelle and the New Rochelle Federation of Teachers, Local 280, AFT,* July 1, 1966–June 30, 1967; *Agreement between the Board of Education of the City of New York and United Federation of Teachers, Local 2, AFT,* July 1, 1965–June 30, 1967; *Agreement between the Newark Board of Education and the Newark Teachers' Association,* July 28, 1965–July 27, 1966; *Contract between the School Committee of the City of Pawtucket and the Pawtucket Teachers' Alliance, Local 930, AFT,* September 1, 1966–August 31, 1969; *Agreement between the Board of Public Education of the School District of Philadelphia and the Philadelphia Federation of Teachers, Local 3, AFT,* September 1, 1965–August 31, 1966; *The Contractual Agreement between the Board of Education of the City School District of Rochester, New York and the Rochester Teachers Association,* July 1, 1965–June 30, 1966.

While the overwhelming majority of the agreements negotiated by the NEA have been in the Level I and II category, the recent tendency has been for Association affiliates in large school districts, Newark, New Haven, Rochester, for example, to press for comprehensive and elaborate documents. In all likelihood, many of those affiliates which settled originally for rather simple and uncomplicated agreements will during the next go-around negotiate with their boards over a greater number of employment conditions. So too, of course, will those AFT affiliates which for one reason or another were unable to secure agreements that provided for anything more than a statement of recognition, a salary schedule, and a grievance procedure, if that much.

In the meantime, if one concentrates on those agreements that have been negotiated by both organizations in the large school systems, one finds that there is little difference in the scope or subject matter of the bargain. The subject matter of agreements in Rochester, New Haven, and Newark, where Associations are the bargaining agents, is in the main no less comprehensive than it is in the contracts negotiated by the Federation in New York City, Boston, and Philadelphia. This conclusion may be verified by a perusal of representative provisions of the New Haven and Boston agreements set forth in parallel columns of the Appendix to this volume.

Similarly, the Newark and New York City agreements have almost identical provisions, which would seem to indicate that the Association in Newark was more sensitive to what had recently happened across the Hudson than whatever recommendations might have been emanating from NEA headquarters in Washington. Both agreements cover salaries, leaves, sabbaticals, relief from non-teaching duties, utilization of teacher aides, assignments, transfers, seniority, class size and number of classes taught, hours of work, the school year, number and duration of faculty meetings, teacher facilities, and a grievance machinery. The New York agreement does provide for binding arbitration (when not prohibited by law or board bylaws), while Newark's is advisory only. This latter difference is less a matter of differing philosophies than it is of differing bargaining environments in local districts. The New Haven contract, for example, negotiated by the Association contains the same kind of binding arbitration provisions as that of the Federation agreement in New York, while in Pawtucket, Rhode Island, the Federation accepted a grievance procedure in its 1966 contract that leaves the school board as the final arbiter.

Of course, from a teacher's point of view the subject matter is less important than the language itself. If the agreement is merely a rewrite of the board's policy manual into contract language, little is gained by collective bargaining. Our impression, after studying several agreements negotiated by both organizations, is that the Federation more often has been able to place a somewhat greater number of restrictions on board prerogatives than has the Association. But this has not always been the case. Thus when the AFT newspaper, *The American Teacher,* chided the Association affiliate in Grosse Pointe, Michigan, for accepting in its contract the clause, "Attendance at and participation in PTA meetings is a normal professional responsibility,"[43] it forgot for the moment that in a contract the Federation had agreed to in Highland Park, Michigan, at about the same time, the PTA obligation read: "It is understood that attendance at a PTA 'Open House' function is *required* [italics added] unless the teacher is excused by the principal."

Since each school district has its own special character, comparing agreements to see which of the two teacher organizations writes the better contracts is a somewhat inexact science. Some boards are tougher and some school districts are poorer than others. On the surface it would appear that the employment conditions negotiated by an NEA affiliate in Rochester are superior, from a teacher viewpoint, to those negotiated by an AFT local in Pawtucket. But this probably says less about the relative strength or viewpoints of the two teacher organizations than it does about the two communities and their school administrations.

We do have one school system, however, New Rochelle, New York, where both teacher organizations have tried their hands at negotiating a collective agreement. The New Rochelle Teachers Association represented the system's teachers from 1964 to 1966; the New Rochelle Federation of Teachers, after winning a representation election in the spring of 1966, negotiated an agreement the following summer.

There are some rather striking differences between the two agreements. In the AFT settlement, salaries were increased substantially: $350 per year for holders of bachelor degrees on step one to a $750 increase for those holding doctorates at step 16. The new agreement established an "Educational Policies Committee" for joint teacher-administration planning on educational policies, curriculum, and other academic matters. The grievance procedure was also changed to conform more closely to the multi-step procedure common in private industry. The Association had bargained for the grievance procedure then being promoted by the NEA which utilized an *ad hoc* screening committee (a committee of peers to judge the merit of each grievance) and specified that, in cases of impasse, a "disinterested person of recognized com-

---

[43] *The American Teacher,* May 1966, p. 7, col. 3.

petence in the field of public education" would render an advisory decision. The final step in the AFT agreement also provides for advisory arbitration, but the arbitrator is to be selected from an American Arbitration Association panel, definitely not an educational channel.

There are other, though less significant, "improvements" — a somewhat more liberal sick-leave policy and a provision for granting in-service credit for teachers who supervise student teachers. There is also at least one setback. Class size, which had been spelled out in the NEA agreement, was now merely to be a subject for "continuing study."

On balance, then, the union seems to have come up with an agreement that better serves the employment interests of New Rochelle teachers. The difficulty with this kind of judgment, however, is that we will never know what kind of agreement the Association might have negotiated had *it* been elected bargaining agent in 1966. As we pointed out earlier, a great many things had happened within the NEA in the intervening two years and, had the New Rochelle Teachers Association been the victor in 1966, it would have been influenced by a different set of precedents from those prevailing in 1964.

Our conclusion, then, guided solely by the scope of the collective agreements negotiated by both teacher organizations, is that there is very little difference between the two when it comes down to the manner in which teachers are to be represented at the local level. In a great many cases, NEA affiliates are beginning to act very much like trade unions. Indeed, when an NEA affiliate participates in a representation election, wins the election and assumes the role of exclusive bargaining agent, enters into negotiations with the employer over a comprehensive agreement, goes out on strike when its terms are not met, wins the strike and administers the agreement with vigor and determination — when an affiliate does all this, it does not seem right to speak of it as anything but a union. Yet increasingly this appears to be the kind of role NEA affiliates are opting to play. The struggle then seems to have become not a contest between rival ideologies, between "professionalism" and "trade unionism," but between rival unions, reminiscent of jurisdictional fights in private employment before the AFL-CIO no-raiding pact.

IV

If the contest between the AFT and NEA, particularly as it manifests itself at the school district level, has indeed become essentially institutional rather than ideological, what purpose is served by perpetuating two teacher organizations? Would not the public school teacher be in a

41

much stronger bargaining position, be able to have greater influence over the educational enterprise, if there were a single teacher organization?

Certainly there are several "public" arguments favoring merger or assimilation, not the least of which is that the competition between the two teacher organizations in some cases has had a divisive effect on the school program. Representation elections, like political elections, require issues and personalities to feed on. And if the issues are bland and the personalities colorless, they are sometimes made to appear controversial and sinister. Campaigns are frequently heated. Teacher organizations hurl charges at one another and on occasion both accuse the board and administration of callousness, if not downright perfidy. Sometimes the organizations feel they must adopt a pose as the most militant of militants. It is of the utmost importance, evidently, particularly in those school systems where the employment relationship has been something less than amicable, that the opposing organization not be allowed to get to one's left. And the best assurance against this eventuality, apparently, is to make charges, demands, and promises that are as extravagant as the opponent's.

The dust of battle settles, but wounds are very often slow to heal. Teachers who fought bitterly in the election campaign are now expected to cooperate on educational and professional concerns. Administrators who were the *bêtes noires* during the campaign are now expected to provide educational leadership to their faculties.

It may have been partly because he was shaken by problems such as these that retiring NEA President Richard Batchelder urged during his presidential address at the 1966 NEA Convention that the two organizations join forces in a single, united teacher organization:

"I . . . invite our colleagues in the AFT to sever ties with labor and unite with the National Education Association so that we can present one common front for the improvement of the teaching profession and can assure that all teachers can serve the needs of all children."[44]

The AFT response was quick but not sympathetic. "We have read with interest your recent public statement that the American Federation of Teachers and the National Education Association form one common front for the improvement of the teaching profession," replied AFT President Cogen. "The AFT stands for a united teacher organization free from administrator domination and dedicated to the improvement

---

[44] Richard D. Batchelder, "Free to Teach," Speech at 104th Annual NEA Convention, Miami Beach, Florida, June 26–July 1, 1966, p. 6.

of American society. Our AFL-CIO affiliation has been a great benefit in pursuing this objective. We therefore have no intention of forsaking our affiliation with organized labor."[45] A month later, at its annual national convention, the AFT again responded to the NEA invitation to join forces by inviting the Association's Classroom Teachers Department to join the union.[46]

So the issue stood as of the fall of 1966. The NEA, although willing to act very much like a trade union at the local level, was adamant that teachers should retain their independence from other social and economic groups. The Kingsport Press issue and the union position on the sales tax were persuasive arguments that affiliation with the labor movement could at times force teachers to take positions that were at odds with high quality education. And, while the NEA seemed to be ridding itself of administration domination or control at both the national and local level, and local affiliates were on occasion striking against these very administrations, a rather heavy emphasis was still put on the community of interest existing among all segments of the profession.

The AFT, on the other hand, profits by its affiliation with organized labor, sees no inconsistency between its AFL-CIO alliance and its professional stance, and is more ideologically attuned to the idea of conflict of interest between teachers and their employers.

There is, moreover, the matter of institutional interests, completely apart from ideological differences, that are served by separation and competition. It has been argued that we have passed the point where this competition serves any real social purpose. But history is replete with examples of institutions that lingered on long after their usefulness had been outgrown. Merger would mean a considerable shuffling of personnel, a loss of status for several of the hierarchy in both organizations, a loss of strongly held institutional identification for thousands of teachers. And, given the intensity of the struggle and the degree of animosity that has been generated by both sides over the last several years, one wonders if either organization is prepared to eat the amount of crow that merger would demand.

Finally, there seems no question that teachers have benefited from this competition. Certainly fewer teachers would be protected by the coverage of a collective agreement had not the AFT challenged the NEA's role as sole guardian of teachers' rights. Competition has moved the NEA to act more militantly, to reassess its obligations to teachers in

---

[45] American Federation of Teachers News Release, June 30, 1966.
[46] *AFL-CIO News,* Sept. 3, 1966, p. 2, col. 1.

their employment capacity, and to press harder at the state and local level for greater teacher benefits. Take away this competition by merging the competitors and a substantial part of the motivation for vigorously serving teachers will have been dissipated.

The public may grow increasingly exasperated at the divisive effect this competition has upon the educational enterprise, just as it may continue to worry about the consequences illegal teacher strikes might have on children's understanding of the importance of law and order. It is likely to be some time, however, before the two organizations will see fit to accommodate their differences. Too much is to be gained by separation.

III

Teacher Bargaining and the Law: Some
Questions and Answers Concerning
Desirable Legislation

FEDERAL AND STATE LABOR LAWS AC-
cording collective bargaining rights to employees of private enterprise
have traditionally excluded employees of government. Not until President Kennedy's Executive Order 10988 of January 17, 1962 expressly
sanctioned such rights for federal employees did any general movement
develop for state legislation granting similar rights to school teachers
and other public employees in the state and local sphere.

Since that executive order, although only partly because of it, the long
pent-up demands of teachers for a greater voice in school affairs have
grown more intense. Old patterns are disintegrating under the pressure.
A frantic effort of state legislatures to cap this pressure and control it
for the public good is now under way. The success of this effort will turn
upon the wisdom of the legislative answers given to the many questions
of law and policy presented. At the time of this writing some eleven states
had enacted legislation pertinent to teacher negotiations, seven of them
in 1965 and 1966. In several other states similar bills had been introduced; but for gubernatorial vetos, bills in Minnesota, New Jersey, and
New York would now be law. It seems a cautious prediction that the
next five years will see many more such enactments. The contours of the
changing employment relations in public education will be significantly
affected in each state by the statutory mold adopted. Since the options
that exist at every turn of the statutory pattern are of crucial concern to
those directly involved — school teachers, school administrators, school
boards — and of grave concern to all others, it makes sense to evaluate
the variety of patterns available.

What are the questions of law and policy that confront the legislator,
and those interested in influencing him, on the subject of teacher bargaining? The major questions are listed below and then discussed.

Questions Concerning Legislation to Govern
the Employment Relationship in Public Education

I. Threshold Questions:

A. Is there any real need for such legislation?

B. If so, should teachers be covered along with other public employees or be singled out for separate treatment?

II. Representation Questions:

A. Determination of the appropriate unit for bargaining:

1. Should supervisory personnel be included?

2. Should "satellite" personnel (e.g. school psychologists, school social workers, school nurses, etc.) be included?

3. Should there be an option on the part of teachers, supervisors, satellite personnel as to whether they want an all-inclusive unit or separate units?

B. Should the question of what teacher organization shall represent a particular unit be determined by an examination of membership lists, authorization cards, petitions, or by a secret election?

C. Who should determine the appropriate bargaining unit and the question of which organization, if any, is the choice of the majority of employees in that unit?

D. Should there be exclusive or proportional representation?

E. How long should the right of exclusive representation last? How often should representation elections be held?

III. Unfair Practices:

A. Should it be an "unfair labor practice" for a school board or administrator to discriminate against employees on the basis of membership or non-membership in an employee organization, or otherwise to interfere with or take part in organizational activities?

B. Should there be a provision requiring either or both the school board and teacher representative to bargain in good faith?

IV. Negotiations:

A. Should the statute merely require *consultation* of the teacher representative by the school board or, instead, provide for actual *bilateral determination* of the conditions of employment?

B. Should the statute indicate the scope or subject matter of negotiations? If so, what should the scope be?

C. Should the statute provide for a written agreement?

D. Should the statute set the duration of the agreement and establish a "contract bar" precluding any challenge of the majority status of the teacher representative during the life of the contract?

V. Strikes, Sanctions, and Impasse Procedures:

A. Should the strike be declared illegal? What of "sanctions," mass "resignations," withholding of "extracurricular" services, "working to rule"?

B. If strikes are declared illegal, what penalties should be imposed?

1. Against individuals?

2. Against employee organizations?

C. What impasse-breaking procedures should be developed?

VI. Administering Agency: Should the law be administered by the state labor board, by the state education department, by a new state agency independent of both the labor board and education department, or on an *ad hoc* basis by mutually selected dispute-resolvers?

. . . .

The eleven states which have thus far provided legislative answers (other than merely banning strikes) to some or all of the foregoing questions can be divided preliminarily into two kinds of groupings.[1] The

---

[1] The full texts of these statutes, with the exception of that of Rhode Island, the most recently enacted, are set forth for convenient reference in T. M. Stinnett, Jack H. Kleinman, and Martha L. Ware, *Professional Negotiations in Public Education* (New York: The Macmillan Co., 1966), pp. 240–268. The full texts of all but the Alaska, Florida, New Hampshire, and Rhode Island statues are also set forth in Myron Lieberman and Michael H. Moskow, *Collective Negotiations for Teachers* (Chicago: Rand McNally & Co., 1966), pp. 448–465.

first dichotomy is between those which merely *authorize* local school boards to bargain or negotiate with teacher representatives and those which *require* such negotiations where the statutory conditions have been met. Three states — Alaska,[2] Florida,[3] and New Hampshire[4] — fall in the former category; the other eight — California,[5] Connecticut,[6] Massachusetts,[7] Michigan,[8] Oregon,[9] Rhode Island,[10] Washington,[11] and Wisconsin[12] — fall in the latter. The second dichotomy is between those states which lump school teachers with other public employees and those which deal with school teachers separately. Five states fall in the former category — Alaska, New Hampshire, Massachusetts, Michigan, and Wisconsin; the other six fall in the latter.

The many other differences between and among these statutes will be commented upon, where pertinent, in the following discussion of the questions previously posed.

I. Threshold Questions

Is there any real need for legislation concerning the collective bargaining rights of public school teachers?

The answer to this threshold question requires a prefatory analysis of the rights possessed by teachers in the absence of an authorizing or mandating statute. Without such legislative approval, do they have (1) the right to organize, (2) the right to negotiate through the teacher organization which represents them, (3) the right to be represented in such negotiations by an *exclusive* majority representative, (4) the right to a *bilateral* determination of their conditions of employment in the form of a collective bargaining agreement duly executed by the majority representative and the school board?

These four questions become increasingly difficult as one moves from the first to the last. As to the right of teachers to organize — i.e. to form and join organizations calculated to further their collective professional

---

[2] *Alaska Stat.* title 23 sec. 23. 40. 010.

[3] *Fla. Stat. Ann.* ch. 230 sec. 230. 23.

[4] *N. H. Rev. Stat. Ann.* 1955 ch. 31 sec. 31.3.

[5] *Cal. Educ. Code* secs. 13080–13088.

[6] *Conn. Gen. Stat. Ann.* title 10 secs. 10–153b — 10–153f.

[7] *Ann. Laws of Mass.* ch. 149 secs. 178G–178N.

[8] *Mich. Stat. Ann.* title 17 secs. 17. 455(1) *et seq.*

[9] *Ore. Rev. Stat.* ch. 342 secs. 342. 450–342. 470.

[10] *Gen. Laws of R. I.* title 28 secs. 28–9. 3–1 — 28–9. 3–16.

[11] *Rev. Code of Wash. Ann.* title 28 appendix 28.6 secs. 1–9.

[12] *West's Wis. Stat. Ann.* ch. 111 sec. 111. 70.

and employment interests — the answer is quite clear. Teachers are presently conceded such a right almost universally, along with any other grouping of Americans, by reason of the First Amendment to the federal Constitution (and the parallel provisions of state constitutions) "protecting the right of the people peaceably to assemble, and to petition the government for a redress of grievances." Indeed, in some thirty-one states, public employees, usually including teachers, have had this constitutional right expressly or implicitly confirmed by statute, court rulings, or attorney general opinions.[13] A handful of states still purport to deny this right to public employees, most frequently directing such proscription against policemen and firemen and, to a lesser extent, teachers. For example, a Georgia statute prohibits policemen from belonging to labor unions;[14] a North Carolina statute has a similar restriction as to both policemen and firemen;[15] in 1963, the Supreme Court of the United States denied review by certiorari of a Michigan Supreme Court decision upholding a regulation prescribed by the chief of police of the city of Muskegon which prohibited policemen from joining "any organization in any manner identified with any Federation or Labor Union which admits to membership persons who are not members of the Muskegon Police Department";[16] a South Carolina attorney general's opinion upheld the validity of a municipal ordinance barring all city employees from union membership;[17] in two early decisions in Illinois[18] and Washington[19] the state courts ruled valid a condition of employment that no teacher belong to a labor union.

While there is something to be said for a limitation on the types of employee organizations which public employees ought to be permitted to join, it seems at this point in our history to be quite clear that blanket attempts to bar them from organizing at all are of most dubious constitutionality. As has been seen, the rights of assembly, association, and petitioning of government for redress, protected by the First Amendment

---

[13] The authorities are gathered in Stinnett, pp. 22–25.

[14] *Code of Ga. Ann.* title 54 sec. 54–909.

[15] *Gen. Stat. of N.C.* ch. 95 sec. 95–97.

[16] Local No. 201, American Federation of State, County and Municipal Employees (AFL-CIO) v. City of Muskegon, 120 N. W. (2d) 197 (Mich. 1963), cert. den. 375 U.S. 833 (1963) (Mr. Justice Douglas was of the opinion that certiorari should have been granted).

[17] Official Opinion No. 641, Annual Report of the Attorney General for the State of South Carolina, 1958–59.

[18] People ex rel. Fursman v. City of Chicago, 116 N.E. 158 (Ill. 1917).

[19] Seattle High School Chapter No. 200, American Federation of Teachers v. Sharples, 293 Pac. 994 (Wash. 1930).

(made applicable by the Fourteenth Amendment to the states and their municipal agencies), entail at minimum the right of self-organization.

Whether such right of self-organization ought to carry with it the right to join *any* variety of employee organization, whatever its character, short of treason, is another question. It is probably already too late, as a practical matter, to raise the question of the wisdom of isolating public employees, including teachers, from organizations of private employees. The present state of teacher organization, as well as of other groups of public employees, argues strongly against such an effort. Nonetheless, thorough analysis can hardly ignore this facet of the organizational problem. The affiliation of public employees with organizations controlled or substantially influenced, whether immediately or ultimately, by organizations of private employees raises the specter of such massive and coordinated employee resistance to government as to cause qualms among all believers in the democratic, rule-of-law experiment still being conducted in this country. The danger is, put minimally, that of reciprocal *economic* back-scratching; put maximally, that of the general, *political* strike from which the United States has thus far been largely, and happily, free.

One way of viewing this problem is to consider a police force organized by, say, the Teamsters. What assurance would there be that such a police force would act in the public interest against private-sector Teamsters engaged in allegedly illegal activities — e.g. unlawful picketing. A related, though lesser, problem exists with respect to public school teachers. To the extent that they are organizationally identified in interest with private-sector employees, to that extent there is the potential that they may take action out of keeping with the public trust reposed in them, as, for example, in honoring picket lines of private employees who happen to have labor disputes situated at the moment on public school premises. The pressure upon government, in the form of the school board, resulting from such action would be, in turn, visited upon the private employer, with potential reciprocity by the private employees (e.g. building construction workers, truck drivers, textbook producers, etc.) whenever the occasion arose. Seeking to deal with this type of threat by outlawing strikes of public employees (including the refusal to cross picket lines) raises enforcement problems not similarly encountered where the protective barrier is raised at an earlier point; the analogy suggested is that of locking the barn after the horse has been stolen.

The concern evinced in the foregoing is probably adequately answered by the argument that public school teachers who are members of an employee organization affiliated with a private-sector organization of employees will have the good sense not to engage in such mutual back-scratching endeavors. Nonetheless, the potential for this kind of reciprocity is greater the more closely affiliated the teacher (or other public employee) organization with organizations of employees in the private sector.

It is pertinent to add that the curtailment of organizational opportunities for public employees, especially policemen, firemen, and perhaps also, teachers, entailed in isolating them organizationally from private-sector employees (perhaps, indeed, even from other groupings of public employees) would not be an obvious violation of their First Amendment rights of free assembly and association. Such restriction as would be involved would, arguably, be the minimum reasonably consistent with the whole scheme of constitutional government: the "soldiers" (employees) of the "sovereign" (the government, the *people*) would be insulated from the pressures of "disloyalty" to the extent consistent with a recognition of their rights to join together for an orderly, lawful presentation of their grievances as public employees.

In any event, the fact is that the patterns of organization of public employees, including teachers, have already crystallized to the extent that a turning back of the clock is probably no longer feasible. We must deal with such organization as it presently exists and is likely to continue to exist and to grow.

As to the right of public school teachers to consult with, to be heard by — i.e. to negotiate with — local school boards *through the teacher organization which represents them,* in the absence of an authorizing or mandating statute, the answer is substantially the same as with respect to their right to organize in the first instance. Again, their right to do so is secured by the freedom of assembly and association and by the cognate right of petitioning their government for a redress of grievances. The right of organization divorced from the right to be heard would be meaningless. And absent the further supportive rights of *exclusive* representation by a teacher organization and of a *bilateral* determination of working conditions, little more is involved in the right to negotiate than the right to be heard. In any event, the present fact is, and has long been, that local school boards do consult with teacher representatives concerning matters of mutual interest; to refuse to do so makes no sense as a matter of personnel administration.

The crux of the question as to whether legislation authorizing or mandating collective bargaining by teachers is necessary is, therefore, not really reached until it is asked whether, absent such legislation, the

51

teachers in a given school district would have the right to be represented in negotiations by an *exclusive* representative chosen by a majority of the teachers involved and whether such majority teacher representative would have the right to demand a *bilateral* determination of working conditions from the school board. It might be contended, with some support from precedent,[20] that a *non-exclusive* teacher representative could demand and obtain bargaining rights on a *members only* basis. But this so flies in the face of the actualities of life as to warrant no more than passing mention; the administrative and statutory problems implicit in having one set of standards and policies (including salaries) for members and another set for non-members make such an approach prohibitive.

The traditional rule is that there is no right on the part of teachers, or any other group of public employees, in the absence of a statute or executive order, to have accorded to a majority representative either exclusive bargaining rights or the cognate right of a bilateral determination of working conditions. It should be clear that the right to exclusivity in bargaining is meaningful only in so far as the school board has a duty to submit questions of employment conditions to bilateral determination; the former without the latter would entail no more than "organized supplication," a condition which the school teachers of this country have tried, found wanting, and are presently rebelling against. This "rebellion" is the frame of reference in which the problems involved are currently presented.

The reason underlying the traditional view, while cast in various terms, is best subsumed under the rubric of "sovereignty." The idea of sovereignty, as the name itself implies, is ancient. It is rooted historically in the concept that the king can do no wrong. Since kings are, with us, passé, so also is the kingly notion of sovereignty. However, there is much more lurking in the concept of sovereignty than merely the divine right of kings. Updated, the residual concern amounts to this: The current sovereign is "the people." This sovereign power expresses itself most fundamentally in a written constitution. Pursuant to this constitution (be it federal or state), power is allocated, on a checks-and-balances basis, to the legislature to make law, the executive to carry out the law, and the judiciary to interpret the law in cases of dispute.

One of the basic notions of this separation-of-powers, this checks-and-balances approach is that power may not be delegated by any one of the

---

[20] See e.g. Norwalk Teachers' Ass'n v. Board of Education of City of Norwalk, 83 A. 2d 482 (Conn. 1951), discussed below.

three branches of government to any other branch or, more specifically for our purposes, to any private repository of power. This rule cannot, of course, be honored absolutely. The legislature cannot, for example, pretend to regulate all segments of our increasingly complex society by statutes nicely tailored to meet every local concern. Accordingly, the legislature creates lesser governmental agencies to deal with specific problems under standards declared by the legislature. One of these "lesser governmental agencies" in the state sphere is the local school board. The local school board, in observance of the foregoing constitutional principles, has only such authority as is expressly or by necessary implication given to it. It follows that the local school board may not itself delegate to private agencies such power as it has been accorded. To do so would be to thwart the sovereign will of "the people," as expressed in their sovereign document, the constitution.

Accordingly, the traditional argument runs, where the local school board (or other agency of government) purports to bind itself, as to future employment conditions, by contract with an organization representing its employees, it has transgressed the authority given to it by the state legislature (pursuant to the basic constitutional covenant), has delegated its own power illegally, and has thereby violated the principle of sovereignty (or of "public policy," as it is frequently called). The local school board has *itself* been constituted to determine such employment conditions; its members have been elected to discharge such trust; *ergo,* to the extent the board has purportedly bound itself by contract to a future resolution of employment conditions, to that extent it has invalidly abdicated the discretion lodged in it alone by the sovereign "people," through their legislative representatives, to exercise a *continuing* discretion, pursuant to statutory standards, with respect to the "superintendence" of school affairs.

There is an undeniable logic to this "sovereignty" view of school administration. There is likewise a brittleness which the current militancy among public school teachers has tested to the point of cracking. The teachers, to the extent they have become organized for something other than "more of the same," have in effect said, "To hell with all of these legalistic arguments; we now have the muscle through organization to get something better than the shabby deal we have been getting for years past, and we hereby *demand* something better!"

Where does all this leave the "sovereignty" argument? In the view of the authors, it leaves the argument at this: The organized demands of school teachers, like those of other public employees, are facts of life which no amount of legal rhetoric can gainsay. These facts of life are the product of a free society, in which the principle of countervailing power is an axiom. The organized teachers have felt their grievances to the extent of gathering their collective strength to deal with them. Their grievances are real; their declaration of them is not neurotic; it makes sense therefore to establish a framework of law within which these grievances, salary and other, may be effectively and legally resolved. This resolution can be fully achieved in any given state only through legislation. Without such legislation, regularizing the exchange of views, there can only be resentment and strife of the sort which a free society can ill afford, particularly with respect to one of its core principles: that its most basic problems can and must be resolved by public education.

In fairness, the question of the propriety of legislation in this area cannot be left without a prediction as to what will follow from it — a significant increase in organizational activity among the school teachers of the particular state, an inpouring of money and manpower from the national organizations in contention for the allegiance of school teachers, and, as a consequence, accelerated change in the relationship of local school boards with the teachers they employ. While this may constitute a "changing of the guard" with respect to the guardianship of public education, it is not at all clear that the change will not be for the better. If the change is for the worse, it augurs ill for the concept of a free society.

This changing of the guard is by no means dependent upon the enactment of legislation authorizing or mandating collective bargaining in the field of public education. The change is proceeding apace across the country regardless of the legislative posture in the particular state. Indeed, the traditional view that a school board, or other governmental employer, may not enter a contract with an organization of public employees covering employment conditions is being rapidly eroded by court decisions, attorney general opinions, and the actual practice of school boards in state after state. It has been reported, for example, that of the 6,000 largest school districts in the United States, 1,661 already have "some form of negotiations, defined as meetings between the superintendent or the board and the teacher organization for 'the express purpose of developing mutually acceptable policies on salaries and/or working conditions.' "[21]

Nowhere has the quality of this change in attitude toward collective bargaining with public employees been more dramatically demonstrated

[21] *Section of Labor Relations Law, American Bar Association, Program of the 1966 Annual Meeting, Montreal, Canada, 1966 Committee Reports,* p. 149.

than in the State of New York. In 1943, the Supreme Court of Albany County declared in *Railway Mail Association* v. *Murphy*:

> To tolerate or recognize any combination of civil service employees of the government as a labor organization or union is not only incompatible with the spirit of democracy, but inconsistent with every principle upon which our government is founded. Nothing is more dangerous to public welfare than to admit that hired servants of the State can dictate to the government the hours, the wages and conditions under which they will carry on essential services vital to the welfare, safety and security of the citizen. . . .
>
> The reasons are obvious which forbid acceptance of any such doctrine. Government is formed for the benefit of all persons, and the duty of all to support it is equally clear. Nothing is more certain than the indispensable necessity of government, and it is equally true that unless the people surrender some of their natural rights to the government it cannot operate. Much as we all recognize the value and the necessity of collective bargaining in industrial and social life, nonetheless, such bargaining is impossible between the government and its employees, by reason of the very nature of government itself. . . .

. . . .

> Collective bargaining has no place in government service. The employer is the whole people. It is impossible for administrative officials to bind the Government of the United States or the State of New York by any agreement made between them and representatives of any union. Government officials and employees are governed and guided by laws which must be obeyed and which cannot be abrogated or set aside by any agreement of employees and officials.[22]

Some thirteen years later, in *Civil Service Forum* v. *New York City Transit Authority*,[23] the New York courts were of a radically different frame of mind. A declaratory judgment was granted upholding the validity of a collective bargaining agreement executed by the Transit Authority and two unions of its employees. The unanimous affirmance by the New York Court of Appeals of the decision in the lower court was rendered without so much as writing a supporting opinion. Two of the seven justices did feel constrained to note in a brief memorandum that they concurred "for affirmance mainly by reason of the limited nature of this contract combined with the history of unionization of this

---

[22] Railway Mail Ass'n v. Murphy, 180 Misc. 868, 875–876, 44 N.Y.S. 2d 601, 607–608 (Sup. Ct. 1943), reversed on other grounds, 267 App. Div. 470 (1944), 293 N.Y. 315 (1944), 326 U.S. 88 (1945).

[23] 3 Misc. 2d 346 (Sup. Ct. 1956), 4 App. Div. 2d 117 (1957), 4 N.Y. 2d 866 (1958).

industry while under private ownership and the presence in the contract of a clause permitting it to be cancelled by the Authority at any time."[24] Part of the "history of unionization of this industry" was that of past strikes. The fact that a decision denying the right of collective bargaining would probably have precipitated another strike was hardly irrelevant to the sharp change in judicial thinking.

Similarly, and perhaps more to the school teacher point, in 1951 the Connecticut Supreme Court of Errors in *Norwalk Teachers' Association* v. *Board of Education,* a landmark decision, answered "yes" to the following question presented to it: "Is collective bargaining to establish salaries and working conditions permissible between the plaintiff [teachers' association] and the defendant [school board]?"[25] The court went on to explain and qualify:

> The statutes...give broad powers to the defendant with reference to educational matters and school management in Norwalk. If it chooses to negotiate with the plaintiff with regard to the employment, salaries, grievance procedure and working conditions of its members, there is no statute...which forbids such negotiations. It is a matter of common knowledge that this is the method pursued in most school systems large enough to support a teachers' association in some form. It would seem to make no difference theoretically whether the negotiations are with a committee of the whole association or with individuals or small related groups, so long as any agreement made with the committee is confined to members of the association. [All but two of the Norwalk teachers belonged to the association.]...The claim of the defendant that this would be an illegal delegation of authority is without merit. The authority is and remains in the board.[26]

The court further added:

> The qualified "Yes" which we give...should not be construed as authority to negotiate a contract which involves the surrender of the board's legal discretion, is contrary to law or is otherwise ultra vires.[27]

It should be noted that this seminal decision, as with the *Transit Authority* case in New York, was rendered in the context of a past strike, which had culminated in the execution of the first collective bargaining agreement between the parties, in April of 1946, and the potential of a further strike in the event that the court had ruled collective bargaining to be beyond the power of the board (as, indeed, it was according to the traditional view).

---

[24] 4 N.Y. 2d at 868, 150 N.E. 2d at 706.

[25] 83 A. 2d at 483 n.l.

[26] *ibid.,* p. 486.

[27] *ibid.*

56

What all of this indicates is simply that law is the product of environment. When the environment changes, the law changes. A rearguard action can be fought by preservators of the status quo, but it is just that — a delaying action. A delaying of inevitable change generates a festering resentment and unnecessary strife. As any student of employment relations in the private sector knows, the most virulent discord occurs where recognition of a majority employee representative for collective bargaining is denied. Such discord can best be avoided in the public education area by a clear-cut legislative mandate to local school boards to bargain collectively with the majority representative of the teachers they employ. Mere authorization to so bargain, as in the case of the Alaska, Florida, and New Hampshire statutes, while a step in the right direction, still leaves to recalcitrant local boards the discretion to thwart the movement of the times. Strikes and related pressures for bargaining rights, whether legal or illegal, will to that extent be fostered, with residual ill will on all sides even after such pressures have achieved their goal. Accordingly, it seems the course of wisdom for state legislatures to resolve the problem in sweeping fashion by mandating collective bargaining where a majority of the teachers in a particular school district has demanded it.

Should teachers be covered along with other public employees or should they be singled out for separate treatment?

The competing philosophies of the two teacher organizations most actively engaged in organizing public school teachers create a natural division between them over this question. The National Education Association is *profession*-oriented, the American Federation of Teachers *employment*-oriented. While both organizations favor state legislation mandating "collective bargaining" or "professional negotiations" between local school boards and an exclusive majority teacher representative, the NEA eschews any statutory scheme which may tend to cause loss of identity of the teaching profession *as a profession*. The AFT, on the other hand, while adhering to the idea of the teacher as a member of a profession, places emphasis on the peculiar character of the teaching profession: teachers, unlike doctors and lawyers, perform their professional functions almost solely as *employees*. They work for an employer (typically a local school board) rather than for private clients, are paid salaries rather than fees, and are subject to the direction and control of "management" as to hours and working conditions in much the same manner as any other employees.

What results from this basic difference of self-image is a whole complex of differences as to approach to the matter of collective negotiations. The very language used to describe the relationships is different. What the AFT calls "collective bargaining," the NEA is apt to describe as "professional negotiations." Similarly, "bargaining units" become "representation units," "exclusive bargaining representatives" become "exclusive negotiating representatives," and so on.

With this background, it may readily be seen why the NEA, concerned with the *professional* image and values, favors completely separate statutory treatment of the "teaching profession." Bunching teachers in with other public employees would tend, it is feared, to dilute the concept of the profession. The AFT, on the other hand, viewing the essential relation between teachers and school boards as one of employment, and being itself affiliated with the AFL-CIO, an international *labor* federation, is much less concerned about teachers being dealt with under a statute covering public employees generally.

Both organizations and their local affiliates lobby actively in the state legislatures for legislation which reflects their image of the teaching profession and their judgment as to its problems and proper solutions. What results in the way of legislation in a particular state is the product of such lobbying efforts (along with the similar efforts of other interest groups — e.g. the AFL–CIO, organizations of school boards and administrators, etc.), the political climate and degree of labor organization, the historical background, and other factors. Frequently, compromise of some sort results, the stronger group politically in the particular state yielding less in the compromise than the weaker group.

As we have seen, of the eight state statutes currently covering public school teachers and mandating (rather than merely authorizing) collective negotiations where the statutory conditions have been met, three cover teachers along with other public employees, whereas the other five deal with teachers separately.

The earliest of these eight statutes, that of Wisconsin, enacted in 1959 and amended in 1962, bestows bargaining rights upon municipal employees, defined as all those ("except city and village policemen, sheriff's deputies, and county traffic officers") employed by a "municipal employer,"[28] the latter in turn being defined as "any city, county, village, town, metropolitan sewerage district, school district or any other political subdivision of the state."[29] A bill enacted by the Wisconsin legislature on

---

[28] *West's Wis. Stat. Ann.* ch. 111 sec. 111. 70(1) (b)
[29] *ibid.,* sec. 111. 70(1) (a).

June 1, 1966, to take effect on January 1, 1967, extends such rights also to *state* employees.[30]

The Massachusetts statute, enacted in 1965, like the Wisconsin statute, covers all employees ("except elected officials, board and commission members, police, and the executive officers") of a "municipal employer," defined as "any county, city, town, or district."[31]

The Michigan statute, enacted in 1965, covers all "public employees," defined as persons "holding a position by appointment or employment" in the state government, in any of the political subdivisions thereof, in the public school service, or in any other branch of public service.[32]

The other five state statutes (California, Connecticut, Oregon, and Washington, all enacted in 1965, and Rhode Island, in 1966) deal with the negotiating rights of public school teachers under statutes covering only certificated teaching personnel.

In the context of what has been said thus far, how persuasive are the arguments for and against separate statutory dealing with school teachers? The arguments *against* may be summarized as follows: It is more efficient, economical, and even-handed to deal with public employees as a group, since this permits the use of the same state machinery and standards for unit determination, conduct of representation elections, adjudication of unfair practice charges, enforcement of antistrike provisions, resolution of bargaining impasses, etc. Moreover, the argument runs, the differences between teachers and other public employees are not as great as the similarities. If special provisions are to be made for teachers, why not also for other groups of public employees, some of whom (e.g. engineers, nurses, social workers) may have comparable claims to singularity, either on the differences-similarities scale or on the professionalism scale? And though teachers are grouped together with other public employees, intelligent administration of such a law would entail distinctive treatment where distinction is properly in order.

The arguments *in favor of* separate treatment, while somewhat more subtle, are also forceful: Teaching has become recognized as a profession because of the acknowledged importance of education to a democratic society. One way such a society seeks to deal with particularly important, sophisticated, and sensitive occupational pursuits is to "professionalize" these callings. This process of professionalization must be encouraged rather than eroded because of the increasingly complex character of

---

[30] *ibid.*, secs. 111. 80–111. 94.

[31] *Ann. Laws of Mass.* ch. 149 sec. 178G.

[32] *Mich. Stat. Ann.* title 17 sec. 17.455(2).

modern society and the concomitantly increasing necessity for higher standards and self-policing of strategic callings. To the extent teachers are treated fungibly with other employees, are dealt with in the matter of collective negotiations by the same agencies, standards, and procedures, to that extent the professionalizing force will be dulled and perhaps ultimately lost. Typical *employee* goals and standards may replace typical *professional* goals and standards, with a stronger tendency to collective protection of mediocrity, even incompetence, as opposed to collective encouragement of aspiration toward excellence, of the seeking of prestige and personal satisfaction through service rather than mere material reward.

The reader's response to these arguments, pro and con, is likely to turn upon the answers he gives to three questions: (1) Is professionalizing a calling an effective way of dealing with society's need for higher standards and dedication in that particular pursuit? (2) If so, is teaching, like law, medicine, and the ministry, properly to be categorized as a profession? (3) If so, is the blanketing of teachers along with other public employees, for the purpose of administering the system of collective negotiations as to the terms and conditions of their employment, likely to derogate from the degree of professionalism teachers currently feel?

To some extent these questions are necessarily tied in with the questions of what agency would administer such blanket legislation and what flexibility of administration, to accord with varying needs and values, could realistically be provided. Further discussion of these questions is postponed, in the interest of economy of treatment, until the consideration of the proper administrative agency is reached in answering the list of questions originally posed.

II. Representation Questions

Should supervisory personnel be included in the bargaining unit for teachers?

Perhaps no question more basically divides the NEA and the AFT than that of whether school principals and other supervisory personnel should be included in teacher bargaining units. In theory, the conflict between the two organizations is irresoluble. In practice, because of the discretion left to local affiliates by each national organization and because of the modifying effect upon each of the growing competition between them, the cleavage is less fundamental.

Since the NEA is profession-oriented, it views all members of the teaching profession, including supervisors and administrators, as part of the same team. The goal of all is the same — the highest possible quality of public education. So viewed, there is harmony, not conflict, of interest between supervisors and supervisees. To divide the team for purposes of collective negotiations, by excluding supervisors from the teacher bargaining unit, is to create an unnecessary and unwise conflict, all to the detriment of the quality of education and therefore of the school children who are the profession's "clients."

The AFT, on the contrary, with its focus upon the *employment* aspect of the teacher's role, views supervisors with the jaundiced eye of organized labor generally. In this view, the supervisor is an adjunct of the employer, management, the "boss." As such, his community of interest is that of the employer, not that of the employees; to recognize this is not to *create* division but simply to *perceive* it. This is, of course, the view long adhered to, and validated by experience in, the private employment sector. The National Labor Relations Act and state labor legislation modeled after it specifically exclude "supervisors" from the definition of "employees" and thereby render them ineligible for membership in employee bargaining units.

There are differences, however, between public and private employment. Indeed, these differences were long a barrier to the whole idea of collective bargaining on the part of public employees. As stated in *Norwalk Teachers' Association* v. *Board of Education*:

> Under our system, the government is established by and run for all of the people, not for the benefit of any person or group. The profit motive, inherent in the principle of free enterprise, is absent. It should be the aim of every employee of the government to do his or her part to make it function as efficiently and economically as possible.[33]

Along with the absence of the profit motive and the consequently diminished motivation for exploitation of public employees by public employers goes a somewhat different quality of relationship between supervisors and supervisees. Wilson R. Hart has commented pertinently upon this difference with respect to federal employees:

> This [composition of the unit] is one area in which there are significant differences between industry and government. The dividing line between labor and management or between workers and super-

33 83 A. 2d at 484.

61

visors is much more clearly drawn in industry than in government. . . .
Both [workers and supervisors in government employment] are covered by the same leave systems, the same pension plans, and the
same operating rules.

Industry is more likely to accentuate the dividing line between the
two categories of personnel by assigning them to different systems and
subjecting them to different company rules. Perhaps as a result of the
different relationship which exists in government, government employee unions have not generally followed the normal trade-union
practice of restricting eligibility for membership to non-supervisory
workers. The only eligibility requirement laid down by most government employee unions is that the member . . . must be on the federal
payroll. Presumably even the President of the United States could
qualify.[34]

Similarly, and even more pertinently, the dissenting opinion in the
decision of May 17, 1966, by the Labor Relations Commission of the
Commonwealth of Massachusetts in a case involving the appropriate
bargaining unit in the public schools of Pittsfield, Massachusetts, had this
to say:

> I reject the theory that the same standards used in industry and
> trade are applicable here in determining what constitutes an appro-
> priate bargaining unit. I find on all the evidence that the supervision
> exercised by principals down to supervisors is not comparable to the
> supervision exercised by supervisors or foremen in industry or trade.
>
> On the one hand, a supervisory employee in industry and trade is
> primarily concerned with the best interests of his employer, and
> usually has the authority to hire and fire other employees. On the other
> hand, principals down to classroom teachers are primarily concerned
> with the proper education of children. They can neither hire nor fire
> subordinates. The authority devolving upon them is not comparable.
> The duties with which principals, vice-principals and supervisors are
> charged is to properly educate students. In order to meet this demand,
> it is vital that all members of this profession operate as a team.
>
> I can find no precedent for holding that members within the same
> profession can be excluded from a unit in which other members are
> admitted. To hold that principals, vice-principals and supervisors
> should be excluded from a unit consisting of school teachers, in my
> opinion would create and perpetuate barriers within the teaching pro-
> fession to the detriment of our children and the profession.
>
> . . . .
>
> I therefore hold that principals, vice-principals, supervisors and
> others, together with classroom teachers, are primarily and funda-

[34] Wilson R. Hart, *Collective Bargaining in the Federal Civil Service* (New
York: Harper & Brothers, 1961), pp. 184–185.

mentally engaged in a profession aimed to educate children, and would constitute an appropriate unit for the purpose of collective bargaining.[35]

The competing views of the NEA and AFT with respect to supervisors are, not surprisingly, reflected in the state laws currently in effect. In states where organized labor is ascendant politically, supervisors are apt to be excluded from teacher bargaining units. Thus, in Michigan, the Public Employment Relations Act, covering teachers along with other public employees and modeled in major respects after the National Labor Relations Act, expressly excludes supervisors from employee bargaining units.[36] Similarly, the Wisconsin statute excludes supervisors.[37] And the Massachusetts statute, expressly excepting only "elected officials, board and commission members, police, and the executive officers of any municipal employer,"[38] has been interpreted by the Massachusetts Labor Relations Commission to exclude principals, vice-principals, and other supervisors.[38a]

In states which have accepted the NEA principle that teachers should not be bunched in with other public employees, but instead dealt with under a separate statute, the situation with respect to supervisors is quite different. The California statute, for example, defines "public school employee" as "any person employed by any public school employer excepting those persons elected by popular vote or appointed by the Governor of this state."[39] Since this statute does not provide for exclusive, but only proportional, representation, there is no occasion to determine appropriate bargaining units. Significantly, however, the statute does provide that "employee organizations shall have the right to represent their *members*."[40] More directly in point, the Oregon and Washington statutes provide for elections among all "certificated" school personnel below the rank of "superintendent" (Oregon)[41] or "chief administrative officer" (Washington)[42] of the local school district to determine

---

[35] City of Pittsfield, Case No. MCR–18, reported in *Government Employee Relations Report* (BNA), No. 168, Nov. 28, 1966, pp. B-2 and 3.

[36] *Mich. Stat. Ann.* ch. 17 secs. 17. 455(13) and 17. 454(10.4).

[37] *West's Wis. Stat. Ann.* ch. 111 secs. 111. 70(4) (d), 111. 02(6), and 111. 02(3).

[38] See n. 31 above.

[38a] This was the decision of the majority in the Pittsfield case, the dissenting opinion of which is quoted in the text accompanying note 35.

[39] *Cal. Educ. Code* sec. 13081(c).

[40] *ibid.,* sec. 13083 (italics added).

[41] *Ore. Rev. Stat.* ch. 342 sec. 343. 460.

[42] *Rev. Code of Wash. Ann.* ch. 28 appendix 28.6 sec. 2.

the exclusive employee representative. On the other hand, the Rhode Island Teachers' Arbitration Act, in maverick fashion, expressly excludes "superintendents, assistant superintendents, principals and assistant principals" "from the provisions of this act."[43]

The Connecticut statute merits special consideration. The product of lobbying compromise between the NEA and AFT, it possesses a unique flexibility. Three varieties of bargaining units are provided for, the variety or varieties to be utilized in a particular school district to be determined by a vote of the personnel involved: (1) a comprehensive unit, including all certificated personnel below the rank of superintendent; (2) a unit excluding supervisory and administrative personnel; (3) a unit restricted to supervisory and administrative personnel. Pursuant to the statutory authorization, all three types of units have been created in the local school districts of Connecticut.

Not only does this flexible arrangement pay service to the democratic principle of self-determination, but also Connecticut has thus provided a laboratory for subsequent study as to the relative merits of inclusion and exclusion of supervisors in teachers' bargaining units. In the judgment of the authors, it is the kind of experimentation which is very much in order at this early stage of teacher bargaining.

Even where agreement can be reached on the principle of excluding "supervisors," there remains the problem of definition. Clearly, the school superintendent and his administrative staff would fall within the supervisory category. The same is true of school principals and assistant principals, at least in the larger school districts. But what of department heads and other lesser "line" personnel in the chain of "command." The statutes which expressly or by interpretation exclude supervisors provide no legislative definition of the term. This leaves the question to the agency which is empowered under the particular statute to resolve such issues. These agencies, as under the Michigan, Wisconsin, and Massachusetts statutes, are typically rooted in private-sector experience, and the strong tendency is to analogize. As stated in a recent decision of the Michigan Labor Mediation Board:

> The term "supervisory employees" is not defined in either the Public Employment Relations Act ... or in the Labor Mediation Act. ... Nor were "supervisory employees" defined in the recent 1965 Amendment to either of the above Acts. The Labor Mediation Board has, by analogy in the past, utilized the definition of the term "supervisor" in Section 2(11) of the National Labor Relations Act, which reads as follows:

---

[43] *Gen. Laws of R.I.* title 28 sec. 28–9. 3–2.

"The term 'supervisor' means any individual having authority, in the interest of the employer, to hire, transfer, suspend, lay off, recall, promote, discharge, assign, reward, or discipline other employees, or responsibility to direct them, or to adjust their grievances, or effectively to recommend such action, if in connection with the foregoing the exercise of such authority is not of a merely routine or clerical nature, but requires the use of independent judgment."[44]

Benjamin H. Wolf, a professional arbitrator called upon by the school board and competing teacher organizations of New Rochelle, New York, for advice as to unit determination in February of 1964, proposed the following definition, which articulates in more simplified fashion the test generally applied in teacher unit determinations where supervisors are excluded: "Supervisors would include those who evaluate the performance of a teacher for the purpose of discipline, tenure or promotion, or whose duties included [sic] the obligation to make recommendations to those who evaluate."[45]

Like most definitions, the foregoing allow of strong difference of opinion in close cases. They also allow of tactical maneuvering in an effort to "gerrymander" the bargaining unit so as to strengthen the chances for victory of one teacher organization at the expense of the other in the ensuing representation election. Thus, in East Detroit, Michigan, the AFT affiliate argued for *inclusion* of "departmental supervisors,"[46] whereas in Grosse Pointe, Michigan, another AFT affiliate sought *exclusion* of "first assistant" teachers (elementary teachers in charge of their buildings when the principal is absent).[47]

All factors considered, the position of the authors· is that the most desirable statutory design for teacher bargaining units is one that allows of sufficient flexibility to permit supervisors to be included in some local school districts and excluded in others. Not enough is yet known on

---

[44] School District of the City of East Detroit, Michigan Labor Mediation Board Case No. R 65 I–49, Jan. 25, 1966. See also School District of the City of Garden City v. Labor Mediation Board, 99 N.W. 2d 485 (Mich. 1959).

[45] "New Rochelle: Advisory Report," *Industrial and Labor Relations Review,* vol. 19, no. 4 (July 1966), p. 576, at p. 577.

[46] See n. 44.

[47] This point was discussed in a paper presented by Donald H. Wollett at the State Leadership Conference on Employment Relations in Public Education, Cornell University, July 14–15, 1966. This paper, along with the others presented at the conference, is published in *Employer-Employee Relations in the Public Schools,* R. E. Doherty, ed. (New York State School of Industrial and Labor Relations, Cornell University, 1967).

this subject to justify the imposition by legislative fiat of an across-the-state inclusionary *or* exclusionary mold. In some districts — smaller, rural ones, for example — the existing "team" feeling of all certificated personnel may be sufficiently strong to make senseless the legislative imposition of divisiveness. In others — perhaps larger, urban districts — the friction caused by existing conflict of interest between supervisors and other teachers may be sufficiently strong to make senseless the legislative imposition of comprehensiveness and cohesion. Perhaps the best way to test the local attitudes is by referendum. For these reasons, the scheme of the Connecticut statute seems wisest. It incorporates the sensible principle of flexibility and protects against mere tactical "gerrymandering" by providing for local self-determination.

Should "satellite" personnel be included in the teacher bargaining unit?

If certificated school personnel are considered for unit-determination purposes as a kind of spectrum, you have at the upper end of the spectrum the question of whether such personnel who are supervisors and administrators should be lopped off, and, if so, at what point of the spectrum the lopping should occur. Next along the spectrum you have the regular, non-supervisory "classroom teacher," as to whom no question of the propriety of inclusion is ever raised. Farther down the spectrum the point is reached where part-time classroom teachers, substitutes, and a whole galaxy of non-teaching but supportive certificated personnel appear. For want of a better term, the latter are here referred to as "satellite" personnel.

Consistent with its view of the professional character of teaching and defining the profession in terms of certification by the appropriate state agency, the NEA supports the inclusion of satellite personnel in the unit. A few local affiliates style themselves as "Classroom Teachers Associations" and for these affiliates a definitional problem may exist. But, by and large, it is accurate to say that the NEA favors a comprehensive unit, encompassing all certificated personnel — i.e. all members of the profession (except superintendents and school board members). Additional arguments sometimes advanced in support of such comprehensiveness are that the bargaining strength of the unit is thus enhanced (more dues payers, etc.), and that it is more efficient and economical in terms of administration not to "Balkanize" the unit, as would be the case if a separate unit or units were to be created for satellite (and supervisory) personnel.

The organizing efforts of the AFT, on the other hand, have been concentrated on classroom teachers, viewed as a kind of craft unto themselves. This has led to AFT resistance to inclusion in *teachers'* bargaining units of *non*-teachers.

Apart from the philosophical differences which divide the two competing organizations, tactical considerations operate strongly to shape their positions regarding the scope of the unit, as to satellite as well as supervisory personnel. In a local situation, the affiliates of each are apt to strive for a unit determination which will maximize the chances of victory in the representation election which follows. Determination of the unit determines also those eligible to vote. Tactics thus merge with philosophy in leading the NEA to contend for an all-inclusive unit; it *organizes* on an all-inclusive basis (frequently, it is sometimes charged, with the help of local superintendents, staffs, and principals). Similarly, the AFT is led to contend for exclusion of non-teaching personnel; it organizes *teachers*.

The existing statutes cast little direct light on the satellite phase of the unit-determination problem. The statutes which deal only with public school personnel seem on their face to resolve the question, but this may be more apparent than real. The Oregon statute, for example, provides for representation by a committee elected for such purpose "by the vote of a majority of the *certificated* school personnel below the rank of superintendent in a school district."[48] The Washington statute is much the same but does expressly define "certificated" employees as those "holding a *regular teaching* certificate of the state and ... employed by any school district with the exception of the chief administrative officer of each local district."[49] The Connecticut statute defines those eligible to vote in representation referenda as "all certificated *professional* personnel below the rank of superintendent, other than *temporary* substitutes, *employed and engaged* either (i) in positions *requiring* a *teaching or special services* certificate or (ii) in positions *requiring* an *administrative or supervisory* certificate."[50] The Rhode Island statute defines those eligible to vote in teacher representation elections as "certified teachers," defining the latter in turn as follows: "certified teachers shall mean certified teaching personnel ... *engaged in teaching* duties."[51]

Anyone who has ever been party to a unit-determination dispute in a

---

[48] *Ore. Rev. Stat.* ch. 342 sec. 342. 460 (italics added).
[49] *Rev. Code of Wash. Ann.* title 28 appendix 28.6 sec. 2 (italics added).
[50] *Conn. Gen. Stat. Ann.* title 10 sec. 10–153(b) (italics added).
[51] *Gen. Laws of R.I.* title 28 sec. 28–9. 3–2 (italics added).

public school system will appreciate the room for lawyerly (and *un-lawyerly*) argument over the *real* meaning of the foregoing statutory language, particularly that which appears in italics. Clearly, school janitors and secretarial help are excluded under any of the foregoing formulations, but what of school nurses, truant officers, school social workers, school psychologists, part-time teachers (both temporary *and* permanent), etc.?

The statutes which bunch school personnel in with other public employees provide even more room for argument on the satellite question. The Massachusetts statute, for example, reads:

> The [state labor relations] commission shall decide in each case whether the appropriate unit for purposes of collective bargaining shall be the municipal employer unit or any other unit thereof; ... provided ... that no unit shall include both professional and non-professional employees unless a majority of such professional employees vote for inclusion in such unit.[52]

The Michigan statute, similarly opaque, incorporates by reference the following procedure tailored for the private sector:

> The [state labor mediation] board ... shall determine such a bargaining unit as will best secure to the employees their right of collective bargaining. The unit shall be either the employees of 1 employer employed in 1 plant or business enterprise within this state, not holding executive or supervisory positions, or a craft unit, or a plant unit, or a subdivision of any of the foregoing units. ...[53]

The situation under the Wisconsin statute is just as obscure, but in a way which deprives the unit-determining agency of any real discretion in the matter. As stated in the 1966 Report of the American Bar Association Committee on the Law of Government Employee Relations:

> The Wisconsin statute, Section 111. 70(4)(d) gives to the [state employment relations] Board very little discretion in establishing the appropriate bargaining units, and requires the Board to conduct a unit election whenever a proposed unit constitutes a division, department, plant or craft of the municipal employer.[54]

Despite the lack of statutory guidance, the strong trend seems to be toward inclusion of satellite personnel in "teacher" bargaining units. Professor George H. Hildebrand, serving as *ad hoc* election "moderator" in the Newark representation dispute, cast light on the reasons for this in

---

[52] *Ann. Laws of Mass.* ch. 149 sec. 178H(4).

[53] *Mich. Stat. Ann.* title 17 sec. 17. 454(10.4).

[54] *Section of Labor Relations Law — 1966, American Bar Association,* p. 177.

his decision of November 23, 1964, establishing "the scope of the unit for voting and representation":

> In deciding upon the inclusion of any occupation, the Moderator brought to bear certain general principles. First, the occupations to be included should share a recognized community of professional interest, one that their incumbents share as employees of the Newark city school system. On this standard, a given occupation either should call for regular teaching assignments, or for directly supportive activities that are clearly and closely associated with teaching as a professional function. . . .
>
> Both organizations [Newark Teachers Association and Newark Teachers Union] agreed at the hearing to the inclusion of the following occupations . . . : *teachers, permanent substitute teachers, itinerant teachers, home-bound teachers, recreational teachers, speech teachers or speech therapists, remedial reading teachers, provisional teachers, guidance counselors, librarians,* and *regular teachers teaching four nights weekly in Newark Evening High School.* . . .
>
> The Moderator also finds that the following additional occupations properly should be included in the unit: *laboratory assistants, coordinators with permanent status as teachers, drop-out counselors, helping teachers, department chairmen who teach at least 50 per cent of their regularly scheduled hours, social workers,* and *psychologists.*[55]

Similarly, Benjamin H. Wolf, *ad hoc* advisor in the New Rochelle dispute, recommended, over the objection of the New Rochelle Federation of Teachers, that guidance counselors, psychologists, social workers, and attendance officers be included in the unit. In explanation of his recommendation, he stated:

> While there is considerable merit in the argument of the Federation and there is historical precedent to support it, I do not consider their view appropriate for New Rochelle. The principal reason is that there are so few in each of these categories, that if they were separated they might have difficulty in organizing for separate representation, and if they did organize, the Board might find itself bargaining with four more sets of representatives, which would be wasteful as to time and unnecessary because there are equally meritorious reasons for including them.
>
> Although these groups do not have identical interests with teachers, they do not have any significant conflicting interests, which was the basic reason for excluding administrators and supervisors, and they do have many parallel and similar interests. All are professionals, certificated by the State Department of Education. They work alongside one another, and their functions dovetail. Most personnel regulations apply

---

[55] Newark: Decision and Opinion of Moderator, *Industrial and Labor Relations Review,* vol. 19, no. 4 (July 1966), p. 587, at p. 588.

to all of them and they are subject to similar supervision. There is considerable historical precedent for combining them. In the field of industrial relations, the industrial unit has become more common than the craft unit.

Where their interests differ, counsellors or psychologists can be members of the teachers' negotiating committee, as is usually the way such problems are handled in industrial units.

There are other communities of interest. Guidance counsellors must have been teachers as a prerequisite to counselling. It is a stepping stone out of the teaching profession and may be regarded as a promotionary step. The Federation representatives frankly admitted that they would accept counsellors if the counsellors wished it. In fact, counsellors, psychologists, social workers and attendance officers are members of the American Federation of Teachers, the Federation's parent body.

My recommendation is that guidance counselors, psychologists, social workers and attendance officers be included in the unit.[56]

The foregoing arguments in support of the inclusion of satellite personnel in teacher bargaining units seem persuasive to the authors. Their persuasiveness to the parties involved in unit determinations is amply evidenced by the satellite-encompassing unit descriptions in many current collective bargaining agreements negotiated by both NEA and AFT affiliates.

Should there be an option on the part of teachers, supervisors, satellite personnel as to whether they want an all-inclusive unit or separate units?

In the opinion of the authors, the answer of the Connecticut statute to this question holds much appeal. Robbins Barstow has explained the procedures adopted pursuant to that statute:

The extraordinary resolution of the problem of unit of representation embodied in Public Act No. 298 is that of *local self-determination within categorically defined limits.* . . .

Three types of representation units, and only three, are provided for under P. A. 298: 1) a unit comprised of all certificated professional employees of the local board below the rank of superintendent; 2) a unit comprised solely of the certificated professional personnel employed and engaged in positions requiring only a teaching or special services (guidance counselor, etc.) certificate; and 3) a unit comprised solely of the certificated professional personnel, below the rank of superintendent, employed and engaged in positions requiring an administrative or supervisory certificate.

---

[56] n. 45 above, at pp. 578–579.

...Only if *both* a majority of the teachers and special services personnel *and* a majority of the administrative and supervisory personnel petition and/or vote for a single, all-inclusive negotiating unit can such a unit be established. If either a majority of teachers or a majority of administrators calls for a separate negotiating unit, such a separate unit must be set up, and the other group has no alternative but to constitute a separate unit itself if it wishes to negotiate under the law. All arrangements are subject, however, to annual review and change.

The machinery devised to implement this unit self-determination provision of the Connecticut law in competing organization towns involves the holding of what is referred to as a *bi-unit* election. A bi-unit election is one in which teachers and administrators take part in a simultaneous election, but each group uses separate ballots in a separate voting place to select a negotiating representative. The same organization or different organizations may be selected to represent each group.

Under the Connecticut statute an election must be held in any school district (but not more than once a year) if a petition is filed with the state commissioner of education by 20 per cent or more of the employees either in the entire group of certificated personnel or in either of the two separate categories. In every instance where petitions for both entire-group and separate-unit elections have been filed in the same town, bi-unit elections have been mutually agreed to. The AAA [American Arbitration Association] has prepared separate ballots for teaching and administrative personnel, with the stipulation that: "In the event the results of the election by both separate units shall result in the election of the same representative organization, such organization shall be declared and certified as the exclusive representative for the entire group, comprising both units, of the certificated professional employees of the board of education."

... In almost all such elections during the first half-year, the choices on the ballots have been, for the teachers: the association, the federation, or neither; and for administrators: the association or "no organization."[57]

As will be noted, the Connecticut statute does not extend the privilege of self-determination to satellite personnel. For reasons previously set forth, this seems, on balance, a sound omission.

Should the question of what teacher organization shall represent a particular unit be determined by an examination of membership lists, authorization cards, petitions, or by a secret election?

All but one of the existing statutes providing for exclusive representation require an election of a majority representative where a question of

[57] Robbins Barstow, "Connecticut's Teacher Negotiation Law: An Early Analysis," *Phi Delta Kappan,* March 1966, p. 345, at p. 349.

representation exists. The exception is the Massachusetts statute which provides: "If, after hearing, the commission finds that there is a controversy concerning the representation of employees, it shall direct an election by secret ballot *or shall use any other suitable method* to determine whether and by which employee organization the employees desire to be represented...."[58]

This means that where there is any real competition between teacher organizations in a local school district, the competition will almost always be resolved by a secret election. Some statutes, indeed, would seem on their face to require an election of a majority representative *whatever* the circumstances may be. This is the case, for example, in Oregon,[59] Washington,[60] and Rhode Island,[61] and (less clearly) Connecticut[62] — all of which have "teachers only" statutes. That these statutes may not mean what a reading of them would suggest is indicated by one of the "Suggestions for Operating under P.A. No. 298" issued by the Secretary of the State Board of Education in Connecticut:

> In the absence of a teacher representation referendum, the board of education may voluntarily enter into arrangements with a teachers' organization or organizations for teacher-board negotiations where there is in the district only one organization which is interested in representing teachers in negotiations or if there is more than one, when these organizations have agreed to seek representation jointly.[63]

As of January 18, 1966, at least 40 Connecticut school districts had granted exclusive representation by a "designation agreement" signed by the local school board on petition of a majority of the certificated professional employees; 23 representation elections had been held.[64]

Similarly, in Michigan, as of the end of February 1966, voluntary recognition (without elections) had been accorded in 376 school districts to NEA affiliates and in 3 districts to AFT affiliates, whereas only 50 representation elections had been held.[65]

---

[58] *Ann. Laws of Mass.* ch. 149 sec. 178H(3) (italics added).

[59] *Ore. Rev. Stat.* ch. 342 sec. 342. 460.

[60] *Rev. Code of Wash. Ann.* title 28 appendix 28.6 sec. 3.

[61] *Gen. Laws of R. I.* title 28 sec. 28–9. 3–5.

[62] *Conn. Gen. Stat. Ann.* title 10 sec. 10–153b.

[63] Part I, sub-part IV B. These "Suggestions" (so-called because the statute does not give any rule-making power to the Secretary of the State Board or any other state agency) were issued on Oct. 20, 1965.

[64] Barstow, n. 57 above, at p. 345.

[65] *Section of Labor Relations Law — 1966, American Bar Association,* p. 163.

The resolution of teacher representation questions by secret ballot elections is eminently sound, since this is the only method by which a *free* exercise of choice can be assured. Reliance upon membership lists, authorization cards, or petitions does not assure the same freedom because of the lack of secrecy and the presence of pressure to conform. Moreover, membership lists are unreliable for the additional reason that many teachers maintain membership in both NEA and AFT organizations (although dual membership is decreasing with the increase in confrontation between the two organizations). Even where dual membership is not present, there is no necessary correlation between membership strength and voting strength. It is not at all uncommon in teacher representation elections for the AFT affiliate to poll more votes than it has current members — sometimes two, three, or more times its membership. This has been true because of the environment in some local school districts favoring membership in the NEA and discouraging it in the AFT, thereby creating a distorted relationship between overt membership and actual preference for purposes of representation.

For these reasons, there is justification for looking askance at *any* formula for according exclusive recognition which does not entail a secret election. The argument in favor of such "voluntary" recognition is, of course, economy — the saving of the time, money, and energy that an election demands. And where there is no request for recognition from a competing organization, the economy argument is forceful. Even here, however, it may be contended that the teachers in the unit should have a free, and therefore *secret,* choice between being represented by the only teacher organization presently in the field and not being represented at all. Such a choice, it may be said, can only be assured by an election. But this is hardly a realistic concern since in a school district where there is no real competition between the NEA and AFT (usually smaller, non-urban districts), the NEA affiliate will almost invariably so dominate the scene as to make an election a mere formality. No force exists in favor of a vote for no representation. The representatives of management (the superintendent and his staff), in all probability NEA members themselves, do not have the same motivation to "campaign" for the "no representation" choice as does the private employer confronted by only one union. Moreover, the NEA is likely to be viewed as the lesser of two evils, and "management" is accordingly happy to have the representation question foreclosed for a period of time via a relatively congenial incumbent.

Perhaps the point of balance to which we are led is that while an election need not be required in every case, the strong presumption should be in favor of an election. The trouble with relying upon this presumption is that the local school board would, in practice, be the prime repository of the discretion to find the presumption rebutted, and the board might choose to grant voluntary recognition in an effort to strengthen the hand of the then dominant organization (in most cases the NEA affiliate).

Several of the existing statutes seek to deal with the question of when an election should be held by providing that a petition be filed with the appropriate agency by the organization seeking recognition, supported by a certain percentage of the employees in the unit sought. Another organization may then intervene, and thereby gain a place on the ballot, by filing its own petition within a designated period of time (usually quite short), supported by a somewhat lesser percentage of the employees in the same unit. Where both such petitions are filed, and found valid, an election is mandatory. Under the Connecticut statute, the two percentages are twenty for the original petition and ten for the intervening petition.[66] Under the Michigan statute, the first percentage is thirty (patterned after the practice of the National Labor Relations Board), and the second is ten.[67] (The 30 percent figure appears in the statute; the 10 percent figure is the product of Michigan Labor Mediation Board policy.) The Massachusetts,[68] Michigan,[69] and Wisconsin[70] statutes also permit the *school board* to petition for a representation election.

The "showing of interest" requirement as a condition to the holding of an election is a sensible one, provided, of course, that proper secrecy is assured to the teachers whose support must be demonstrated to the appropriate agency. For this reason, among others, the latter agency should not be the local school board.

Who should determine the appropriate bargaining unit and the question of which organization, if any, is the choice of the majority of employees in that unit?

This question, while vital to a full consideration of representation problems (as evidenced, for example, by the last paragraph of the

[66] *Conn. Gen. Stat. Ann.* title 10 sec. 10–153b(b).

[67] *Mich. Stat. Ann.* title 17 sec. 17. 455(12) (a); *Section of Labor Relations Law — 1966, American Bar Association,* p. 146.

[68] *Ann. Laws of Mass.* ch. 149 sec. 178H(2).

[69] *Mich. Stat. Ann.* title 17 sec. 17.455(12) (b).

[70] *West's Wis. Stat. Ann.* ch. 111 sec. 111. 70(4) (d).

preceding section), can be dealt with more economically through postponing discussion until the broader, encompassing question of the proper administering agency for teacher bargaining in general is reached.

Should there be exclusive or proportional representation?

This question, in the judgment of the authors, does not merit belaboring. If what is desired is a *bilateral* determination of the conditions of employment (as opposed to the traditional *unilateral* determination of such by the school. board, with or without mere "consultation"), it seems patently evident that an exclusive representative to conduct the teachers' side of the two-sided determination is in order. Proportional representation, as the name itself makes clear, divides the representation on the teachers' side, transfers to the bargaining table the competition of views between the contending teacher organizations instead of resolving them at the representation stage, and thereby impairs the process of reaching agreement through collective negotiations.

To the extent that proportional representation weakens the solidarity of teachers at the bargaining table (as, of course, it does), it may be favored by some school boards, clinging to traditional prerogatives and welcoming for this purpose the strategy of "divide and conquer." There is strong reason to believe, however, that in any school district where one teacher organization is not overwhelmingly dominant, and where, as a consequence, proportional representation would not approximate, *in practice,* exclusive representation, the school board would "reap the whirlwind." Every (tripartite) meeting of the negotiators would hold the potential of a donnybrook. Confidential exchanges of views would be most difficult because the representatives of the minority teacher group present would be alert to carry from the conference table any available ammunition in the continuing battle to win adherents from the majority group's camp. The position of the superintendent of schools would be even more precarious and unenviable than it is sometimes represented to be where the principle of exclusive representation is recognized. Instead of answering to one set of teacher representatives, he would be confronted by two, each set possessed of perpetually recognized standing to call him and his policies to account. Even where his and the board's policies are sound, the competing political forces institutionalized by proportional representation would lead to a maximizing of the negative as political advantage dictated.

This is a poor way to run a shop, as the experience in the private sector, where exclusive representation is universally honored under federal and state statutes, makes abundantly clear. Little reason, if any, appears for distinguishing the public shop from the private shop in this regard. Indeed, the existing statutes covering school teachers all recognize the wisdom of exclusive representation, with the sole exception of California.

The California statute provides:

> An employee organization representing certificated employees shall be entitled to appoint such number of members of the negotiating council [which "shall have not more than nine nor less than five members"] as bears as nearly as practicable the same ratio to the total number of members of the negotiating council as the number of members of the employee organization bears to the total number of certificated employees of the public school employer who are members of employee organizations representing certificated employees.[71]

It is significant that the California statute does not provide for a bilateral determination of conditions of employment. Nor does it provide for any written agreement. What it does provide for, and *all* it provides for, is the right of employee representatives to "meet and confer" with the public school employer or its designated representatives.[72]

The 1966 Report of the Committee on the Law of Government Employee Relations of the ABA Section of Labor Relations Law makes this comment on the California statute:

> Evidence to date on the operation of the law in school districts in California is inconclusive. Negotiating councils (with little AFT representation) are operating throughout the state. However, no bilateral, written agreements of any consequence between teacher organizations and boards of education have yet been negotiated, and none are required by statute.[73]

The reason for the "little AFT representation" on the negotiating councils is that many of the local AFT affiliates have boycotted the councils.

Significantly, *both* national teacher organizations espouse the principle of exclusive representation, although the NEA is a rather late convert, initially repelled by the labor (rather than professional) origin of the concept, but finally won over by more intimate experience with collective negotiations in a context of strong competitive pressure from the AFT.

---

[71] *Cal. Educ. Code* sec. 13085.

[72] *ibid.*

[73] *Section of Labor Relations Law — 1966, American Bar Association*, p. 151.

While the very dynamics of collective bargaining establish the case for exclusive representation, one difference between the private and public sectors in the application of the principle should be noted. The opinion has recently been expressed that:

> Since boards of education are public bodies, they cannot deny a hearing to minority employee organizations or individuals. When the organization representing the majority is accorded exclusive negotiation rights, the minority organizations and individuals must be guaranteed testimony rights. That is, they must be given the opportunity to present views to the governing board. If testimony rights are protected, there is nothing illegal in the board's negotiating with the majority organization exclusively, so long as the results of the negotiations apply equally to all the professional staff, regardless of membership or nonmembership in the organization representing the majority.[74]

How long should the right of exclusive representation last? How often should representation elections be held?

As we have seen, the purpose of determining by a secret ballot election what organization shall be the exclusive representative is to assure freedom of choice to the teachers in the bargaining unit. But this freedom of choice must be limited to the extent necessary to achieve reasonable stability in the bargaining relationship. In other words, the organization which wins a representation election should be allowed a reasonable time in office before being subjected to the challenge of a new election by the competing organization. This accommodation of freedom of choice and stability of relationship is achieved in the private sector, under federal and state labor relations acts, through the application of "election bar" and "contract bar" rules.

For example, under the National Labor Relations Act a valid representation election serves as a bar to another election for a period of one year.[75] This means that the employee organization which wins such an election is assured of one year's time, free of the necessity of reestablishing its majority status, during which to seek to negotiate a contract. If a contract is negotiated during the year, the contract, in turn, becomes a bar to any further representation proceedings for the period of its life, up to a maximum of three years.[76]

We will have occasion in a subsequent section to discuss the "contract

---

[74] Stinnet, p. 42.

[75] Labor-Management Relations Act (Taft-Hartley Act) sec. 9(c) (3), 61 Stat. 143 (1947), 29 U.S.C. sec. 159(c)(3) (1964).

[76] General Cable Corp., 139 NLRB 1123 (1962).

bar" as applied to school teachers. At this point, the focus is on the "election bar."

Express election bar provisions are found in four of the existing teacher bargaining statutes. The Massachusetts statute, for example, provides: "No election shall be directed in any bargaining unit . . . within which in the preceding twelve-month period a valid election has been held."[77] The language of the Michigan statute is substantially the same.[78] The Connecticut statute is only slightly variant: ". . . not more than one such referendum shall be held in any one school year."[79] The Rhode Island statute contains the usual language but adds a provision which has particular significance for school teacher bargaining: "Elections shall not be held more often than once each twelve months and must be held at least thirty (30) days before the expiration date of any employment contract."[80]

The last clause of the foregoing is apparently designed to deal with the problem of budgetary deadlines in school teacher (and other public employee) bargaining. Such deadlines present one of the most troublesome differences between public-sector and private-sector bargaining. The problem arises in this fashion. The budget of a local school district must be prepared and approved under the law of the state by a certain date. This date usually occurs sometime in the spring, geared to the expiration of the current individual employment contracts of the teachers in the district. The new budget is, of course, for the following school year.

The existence of these budgetary deadlines under state law places great pressures of timing on teacher bargaining. Since salaries and other economic matters are apt to be the core issues at the bargaining table, negotiations must be initiated far enough in advance of budgetary deadlines to give reasonable assurance that agreement may be reached before the deadline. The problem is accentuated where there is a petition for a new election challenging the right of the existing majority representative to continue in that capacity. The very filing of such a petition has, of course, a substantial impact upon the negotiations then in progress between the incumbent representative and the school board. Indeed, it may bring such bargaining substantially to a halt.

The disruptive effect of the filing of a petition for a new representation election has been recognized by the National Labor Relations Board,

---

[77] *Ann. Laws of Mass.* ch. 149 sec. 178H(3).

[78] *Mich. Stat. Ann.* title 17 sec. 17. 455(14).

[79] *Conn. Gen. Stat. Ann.* title 10 sec. 10–153b(b).

[80] *Gen. Laws of R.I.* title 28 sec. 28–9. 3–7.

in the private sector, and administratively compensated for by rules requiring such a petition to be filed no more than ninety days nor less than sixty-one days before the expiration of the existing contract.[81] Once a timely and otherwise valid petition has been filed, the right of the incumbent representative and the private employer to execute a new contract is suspended until the election has been held and the results certified. After this, negotiations may begin anew between the private employer and the employee organization which wins the election.

A moment's thought will reveal the complications for this process which the budgetary deadlines pose in the public employment sphere. The timing of the representation election must be such as to allow a sufficient period after the election for a new contract to be negotiated by the victorious teacher organization *prior to* the budgetary deadline date. If this timing is not achieved, the teachers in the unit could be effectively deprived of a reasonable opportunity to negotiate on the core money issues for an entire school year.

Accordingly, considerable attention should be paid to this problem of election timing in the legislating and administering of teacher bargaining laws. None of the existing statutes seems to have taken this problem adequately into account, leaving it apparently to administrative resolution.

There is no one statutory formula which can answer the problem of election timing in every state, since the laws of the states vary on school district budgetary deadlines. Indeed, in states such as New York which have both dependent and independent school districts, the problem of budgetary deadlines is further complicated by the fact that different deadlines exist for each. The dependent school district must first meet its own budgetary deadline, and then the budgetary deadline of the city council, to which the school district budget must be presented for inclusion in the total city budget, must in turn be met.

The authors do, however, suggest one statutory palliative which experience to date appears to support. This is that the election of teacher representatives be limited to once every *two* years. Not only would this reduce the problem presented by budgetary deadlines, but, perhaps even more important, it would afford a much better opportunity for the school board and a new teacher representative to work out a stable, desirable relationship without derogating unduly from the freedom of choice of representative on the part of the teachers.

---

[81] Leonard Wholesale Meats, Inc., 136 NLRB 1000 (1962).

Some dissent might be registered to this proposal on the score that if neither competing teacher organization won the election, but instead the bargaining unit voted for no representation (the third choice on teacher ballots), an election bar of two years would be too long, since it would deny any representation for the entire period. However, the statutory election bar could be framed in such terms as to constitute a two-year bar *only* where one of the competing organizations prevailed; if the vote were for no representation, the bar would be for one year only. Moreover, the experience to date with teacher representation elections indicates that one of the competing organizations invariably prevails.

III. Unfair Practices

Should it be an "unfair labor practice" for a school board or administrator to discriminate against employees on the basis of membership or non-membership in an employee organization, or otherwise to interfere with or take part in organizational activities?

The corollary of acknowledging the right of school teachers to organize and to bargain collectively is to create a duty on the part of those in a position to interfere with these rights — viz., school boards and administrators — not to so interfere. The legislative creation of the rights would imply the duties even if the latter were not expressly stated. For the sake of clarity and the mutual understanding of teachers and school administrators, it is wise to spell out the duties as well as the rights. This is the course followed by federal and state labor relations acts with respect to private enterprise. The National Labor Relations Act establishes certain unfair labor practices on the part of employers. For present purposes, the most pertinent are: (1) discrimination in terms or tenure of employment to encourage or discourage membership in an employee organization, (2) interference with, restraint, or coercion of employees in the exercise of their rights to organize and bargain collectively.[82]

Six of the eight current statutes mandating teacher negotiations speak expressly to the matter of such discrimination and interference by school administrators. As might be expected, the Massachusetts, Michigan, and Wisconsin statutes, which lump teachers in with other public

---

[82] Labor-Management Relations Act secs. 8(a) (3) and (1), 61 Stat. 140 (1947), 29 U.S.C. secs. 158(a) (3) and (1) (1964).

employees under a statutory scheme analogous to the National Labor Relations Act, cover this matter most thoroughly. The Michigan statute, by way of illustration, provides:

> It shall be unlawful for a public employer or an officer or agent of a public employer (a) to interfere with, restrain or coerce public employees in the exercise of their rights guaranteed in section 9 [to organize, bargain collectively, and engage in lawful concerted activities]; (b) to initiate, create, dominate, contribute to or interfere with the formation or administration of any labor organization . . . ; (c) to discriminate in regard to hire, terms or other conditions of employment in order to encourage or discourage membership in a labor organization; (d) to discriminate against a public employee because he has given testimony or instituted proceedings under this act. . . .[83]

Violations of any of these provisions are "deemed to be unfair labor practices remediable by the labor mediation board."[84] In line with the National Labor Relations Act, after which the procedures are modeled, provision is made for the issuance of complaints, a hearing before a trial examiner, administrative review by the board, and judicial review in the state courts. The board is empowered, where an unfair labor practice has been found to have been committed, to issue a "cease and desist" order and "to take such affirmative action including reinstatement of employees with or without back pay, as will effectuate the policies of this act."[85]

The Rhode Island statute, though confined to teachers, has unfair labor practice procedures paralleling the Michigan, Massachusetts, and Wisconsin acts. In the following language, it incorporates by reference the provisions of the Rhode Island statute covering private employees:

> Complaints of interference, restraint, discrimination or coercion shall be heard and dealt with by the labor relations board as provided in chapter 28–7 of this title. All unfair labor practices enumerated in section 28–7–13 are declared to be unfair labor practices for a school committee.[86]

The California and Connecticut statutes, both restricted to teachers, prohibit certain practices but specify no agency or procedures for enforcement of the prohibitions. Presumably, enforcement is left to the state courts. The California statute reads: "Public school employers and

---

[83] *Mich. Stat. Ann.* title 17 sec. 17. 455(10).

[84] *ibid.*, sec. 17. 455(16).

[85] *ibid.*, sec. 17. 455(16) (b).

[86] *Gen. Laws of R.I.* title 28 sec. 28–9. 3–6.

employee organizations shall not interfere with, intimidate, restrain, coerce or discriminate against public school employees because of their exercise of their rights under Section 13082."[87]

The Connecticut statute contains an interestingly detailed "equal treatment" provision. It reads:

> The local or regional board of education, and its representatives, agents and superintendents shall not interfere [sic], restrain or coerce employees in the rights guaranteed by [this act], and, in the absence of any certification as the exclusive representative ... all organizations seeking to represent members of the teaching profession shall be accorded equal treatment with respect to access to teachers, principals, members of the board of education, records and participation in discussions with respect to salaries and other conditions of employment.[88]

A recent decision of the Michigan Labor Mediation Board, under a statute less explicit than the Connecticut statute with respect to "equal treatment," reached an accordant conclusion. The decision states:

> It is established that on three separate dates agents of the Employer permitted representatives of the Association to solicit support or membership at faculty meetings. Employee attendance at these meetings was compulsory. However, there is no corresponding evidence that the Federation was denied, or even requested, equal opportunity to present its views or distribute its authorization cards at these faculty meetings. Failure of one of two competing groups, for reasons of its own, to avail itself of an opportunity to campaign does not automatically render illegal the Employer's conduct in permitting the other group to take advantage of such an opportunity. [NLRB citations omitted.]
>
> Nevertheless, it is manifest from this record that the Employer has so restricted the campaigning activities of the Federation, while at the same time accommodating the interests of the Association, as to create a serious imbalance in organizational opportunities between the two groups. Thus, while publicizing Association meetings, permitting Association agents to freely campaign both at faculty meetings and during working hours, and permitting Association literature to be displayed on a bulletin board in the Board of Education offices (none of which acts is *per se* unlawful), the Public Employer here impeded the Federation's circulation of its literature to newly-employed teachers. Such disparity in treatment of rival organizations during an election campaign constitutes improper assistance to the Association and interference with employees in the exercise of their self-organizational rights guaranteed in Section 9 of the Act. [NLRB citations omitted.]

---

[87] *Cal. Educ. Code* sec. 13086.
[88] *Conn. Gen. Stat. Ann.* title 10 sec. 10–153d.

The Public Employer's recently-promulgated policy prohibiting the distribution, *without prior approval,* of *any* material to the teachers' mail boxes in the school buildings or via the inter-school mail delivery system, although not discriminatorily applied against the Federation, is nonetheless attacked as interference with the organizational activities of both groups, insofar as it is applied to campaign literature. Constitutional and public policy issues involving prior censorship of reading matter by an agency of the state may be present here. However, I shall refrain from commenting on such issues, limiting this analysis to the effect of such a restrictive rule upon organizational opportunities in the public school environment.

Weighing the potentially disruptive effect of widespread distribution of campaign literature to teachers outside the school buildings or in the hallways, and the obvious orderliness of distribution of literature via the teachers' mail boxes and the inter-school mail delivery system, the undersigned is persuaded that a school rule prohibiting the use of such means of communication, without the employer's approval, constitutes interference with, and restraint of, the employees in the exercise of their Section 9 self-organizational rights, absent a showing of special circumstances justifying such a rule. While an employee should not have to reveal his organizational sympathies by obtaining prior approval before distributing literature or membership cards in the teachers' mail boxes on his own time, it is noted that the employer may still properly forbid distribution of such materials by employees during their working hours.[89]

Although the foregoing passages from this Michigan decision are instructive, they leave unanswered the important question of the extent to which the public employer should be allowed itself to campaign for the teacher organization which it prefers. The employer "free speech" provision of the National Labor Relations Act,[90] of course, protects this interest in the case of private employers. A later passage of the same Michigan decision indicates that in that state a fairly complete analogy between public and private employers has been recognized:

Several members of the Employer's administrative and supervisory staff have worn pins and insignia of the Association, presumably during the election campaign. Additionally, an Association sticker has remain [*sic*] posted on one principal's office door since September, 1965. While this tends to show that some of the Employer's supervisors and agents belong to, or at least prefer, the Association, such evidence

[89] Utica Community Schools, Michigan Labor Mediation Board Case No. C66–B–9, June 1, 1966.

[90] Labor-Management Relations Act sec. 8(c), 61 Stat. 140 (1947), 29 U.S.C. sec. 158(c) (1964).

of personal preference does not amount to a violation of the Act, since the employer is free to indicate its preference between competing organizations, absent threats or promises of benefit.[91]

This solution to the employer free speech question seems sound, qualified as it is by the requirement that the employer's words and actions be free of elements of coercion or promises of benefit. Indeed, any other resolution might entail constitutional questions under the First Amendment. But the test of law is not always the test of wisdom. School boards and administrators would hardly be well advised to enter the lists in a representation contest on the side of either teacher organization. The ill will that would be thus engendered would be self-defeating. Nor would it make sense for them to campaign for "no representation" (the goal of most private employer exercise of free speech); experience demonstrates the futility of this third choice on teacher representation ballots.

Moreover, to the extent school boards and administrators maintain other than a strict neutrality in teacher representation disputes they provide the wherewithal for the filing of unfair practice charges, however frivolous, with resulting expenditure of time, money, and energy in the litigation of such charges. The tactical potential of such charges to delay elections for the purpose of facilitating last-minute vote drives is illustrated by the early experience in Michigan, as reported by Robert G. Howlett, chairman of the Michigan Labor Mediation Board:

> Efforts to delay elections have been present primarily in the education area, where there is vigorous competition between MEA and MFT affiliates. School officials are understandably concerned because they are preparing 1966–67 budgets, and as long as there is no determination as to which of the two groups is bargaining agent, school boards are not in a position to intelligently allocate funds. Under the well-established rules of the NLRB, as well as MLMB cases in private industry, working conditions may not be changed, after demand for recognition, until a bargaining agent is determined, or the employees decide they do not wish one. With the upward trend of teachers' salaries and the teacher shortage, school boards, if they cannot increase salaries, may find themselves in difficulty for the 1966–67 school year.
>
> To help alleviate this situation, we adopted, over objection by some union attorneys, a policy of scheduling unfair labor practice hearings and representation hearings together, with the evidence on the representation petition being taken immediately at the close of the testimony

---

[91] n. 89 above.

on the unfair labor practice. Thus, if unfair labor practice charges are dismissed, the Board is in a position to proceed with the election.[92]

While this procedure has considerably reduced the opportunity for stalling elections by the filing of tenuous unfair labor practice charges, it has not, Howlett reports, "prevented the Board members from receiving several dozen letters from irate teachers and school officials protesting delay. Some even complained to the Governor."[93]

Should there be a provision requiring either or both the school board and teacher representative to bargain in good faith?

If the statute gives a right to teachers to bargain collectively with their school employer over conditions of their employment, the corollary of this right is a duty on the part of the employer to so bargain. The content of this duty is best expressed as a good faith effort to reach agreement. If the content of the duty is more strongly expressed — e.g. a *reasonable* effort to reach agreement — there is an infringement upon the freedom of the bargaining. If the content of the duty is less strongly expressed — e.g. merely to "meet and confer" — there is no protection against sham bargaining. In the effort to avoid sham bargaining without unduly impinging upon the freedom of bargaining, the National Labor Relations Act has cast the private sector bargaining duty in terms of "good faith."[94]

All but one of the statutes which purport to grant the right of collective bargaining to teachers likewise impose the correlative duty on school boards to bargain in good faith. Thus, the Connecticut statute provides:

> The local or regional board of education and the organization designated as exclusive representatives for the appropriate unit, through designated officials or their representatives, shall have the duty to negotiate with respect to salaries and other conditions of employment, and such duty shall include the obligation of such board of education to meet at reasonable times, including meetings appropriately related to the budget-making process, and confer in good faith with respect to salaries and other conditions of employment, or

---

[92] The quotation is from a paper presented by Chairman Howlett in March 1966 at a conference on Public Employment and Collective Bargaining held at the University of Chicago's Center for Continuing Education. The title of the paper is "Problems of a State Public Employment Relations Law in Practice."

[93] *ibid.*

[94] Labor-Management Relations Act sec. 8(d), 61 Stat. 140 (1947), 29 U.S.C. sec. 158(d) (1964).

the negotiation of an agreement, or any question arising thereunder and the execution of a written contract incorporating any agreement reached if requested by either party, but such obligation shall not compel either party to agree to a proposal or require the making of a concession.[95]

The Massachusetts,[96] Michigan,[97] and Rhode Island[98] statutes are to similar effect. The Rhode Island statute does, however, attempt to take into account the troublesome matter of budgetary deadlines in specific fashion by providing:

Whenever salary or other matters requiring appropriation of money by any city, town or regional school district are to be included as matter of negotiation or collective bargaining conducted under the provisions of this chapter, the negotiating or bargaining agent must first serve written notice of request for negotiating or collective bargaining on the school committee at least one hundred and twenty (120) days before the last day on which money can be appropriated by the city or town to cover the first year of the contract period which is the subject of the negotiating or bargaining procedure.[99]

The California, Oregon, and Washington statutes, while acknowledging the right of teachers to engage in collective discussions with school employers concerning conditions of employment, do not really grant the right to bargain collectively. Accordingly, there is no occasion for them to deal with the correlative duty of the school employer to *bargain*. The language of these statutes varies, but what they accord is merely the right of *consultation*, the power of *decision* being left to unilateral determination by the school board.

Thus, the California statute provides that "a public school employer or the governing board thereof, or such administrative officer as it may designate, shall meet and confer with representatives of employee organizations upon request. . . ."[100]

The Washington statute provides:

Representatives of [the majority] employee organization . . . shall have the right, after using established administrative channels, to meet, confer and negotiate with the board of directors of the school

---

[95] *Conn. Gen. Stat. Ann.* title 10 sec. 10–153d.
[96] *Ann. Laws of Mass.* ch. 149 secs. 178I and L.
[97] *Mich. Stat. Ann.* title 17 sec. 17. 455(10) and (15).
[98] *Gen. Laws of R.I.* title 28 sec. 28–9. 3–4.
[99] *ibid.*, sec. 28–9. 3–8.
[100] *Cal. Educ. Code* sec. 13085.

district or a committee thereof to communicate the considered professional judgment of the certificated staff prior to the final adoption by the board of proposed school policies. . . .[101]

And the Oregon statute similarly provides:

> Certificated school personnel, individually or by a committee [elected by a majority vote] . . . shall have the right to confer, consult and discuss in good faith with the district school board by which they are employed, or a committee thereof, on matters of salaries and related economic policies affecting professional services.[102]

The one real curiosity among the existing statutes with respect to the duty to bargain is the Wisconsin statute. While the statute grants collective bargaining rights and is patterned in several respects after the National Labor Relations Act, it does not (as with the similar Massachusetts and Michigan statutes) lay down any duty to bargain in good faith. Nor does it ignore the matter completely. Instead, it provides:

> *Fact finding.* Fact finding may be initiated in the following circumstances: 1. If after a reasonable period of negotiation the parties are deadlocked, either party or the parties jointly may initiate fact finding; 2. Where an employer or union fails or refuses to meet and negotiate in good faith at reasonable times in a bona fide effort to arrive at a settlement.[103]

Interpreting the foregoing provision in a recent case, the Wisconsin Board, in a 2–to–1 decision, held that the Wisconsin statute did *not* make it a prohibited practice for a municipal employer to refuse to bargain. The majority opinion stated:

> It would appear to us that had the legislature intended that a refusal to bargain in good faith in public employment should constitute a prohibited practice, it would have specifically provided for same in the statute. . . .[104]

The sole relief, according to the majority, for such a refusal to bargain was to file a petition initiating fact finding. (The "fact finder" under the Wisconsin statute is appointed by the state labor board and empowered to hold hearings and make recommendations.)[105]

---

[101] *Rev. Code of Wash. Ann.* title 28 appendix 28.6 sec. 3.

[102] *Ore. Rev. Stat.* ch. 342 sec. 342. 460.

[103] *West's Wis. Stat. Ann.* ch. 111 sec. 111. 70(4) (e).

[104] City of New Berlin, Dec. No. 7293, March 1966, quoted in *Section of Labor Relations Law — 1966, American Bar Association,* p. 179.

[105] *West's Wis. Stat. Ann.* ch. 111 secs. 111. 70(4)(f) and (g).

The dissenting opinion cogently argued:

> If the Legislature has granted to municipal employes the legal right to engage in collective bargaining, as I believe it has done, it necessarily follows that a corollary of such right is the duty to "bargain" or "negotiate" with the majority representative of its employes. If there be no legal duty on the municipal employer to bargain with the representative selected by its employes, then how can the employes be said to have a right to bargain? To ask the question is to answer it....[106]

In defense of this Wisconsin decision it may be said that, even if the employer had bargained in good faith but still no agreement could be reached, the only resort of the employee representative would have been to fact finding, as provided by the statute; therefore, since fact finding was available anyway for the refusal to bargain, no real loss resulted to the employees. The difficulty with this reasoning is that fact finding and similar impasse-resolving procedures are, at best, poor substitutes for the settlement of differences through mutual agreement. The strength of collective bargaining lies in the greater *acceptability* of the accord it produces, as compared to a settlement sought to be imposed by third parties. Where no effective duty to bargain is enforced, resort may be increasingly had to the fact-finding alternative; collective bargaining decays, and fact finding (never yet demonstrated to be a sustained success in other collective bargaining areas) is left to bear a weight difficult to support.

In view of the desirability of minimizing to the extent possible the resort to fact finding (of which more will be said in a subsequent section), the public employer should be placed under the duty to bargain in good faith, enforceable before a designated administrative agency (as in Massachusetts, Michigan, and Rhode Island) or in the courts (as, apparently, in Connecticut, where the statute is silent as to the means of enforcement). And since bargaining is a two-way process, the same duty should be placed upon the employee representative, as is the case in Connecticut, Massachusetts, Michigan (although not expressly made an unfair labor practice for the employee representative, as it is for the employer), and Rhode Island. If both parties understand that they have this legal duty to bargain in a good-faith effort to reach agreement, the potential of collective bargaining to enhance employment harmony in public education will be maximized. Conversely, the necessity for resort to impasse-resolving techniques will be minimized.

---

[106] n. 104 above.

IV. Negotiations

Should the statute merely require consultation of the teacher representative by the school board or, instead, provide for actual bilateral determination of the conditions of employment?

School districts in states which have not yet mandated collective bargaining have been energized by the current teacher "rebellion" to reconsider their traditional practices with respect to personnel administration. The result has been a resort to new or revitalized procedures which afford teacher representatives an opportunity to be heard concerning questions of salaries, other employment conditions, and school policy. In the opinion of the authors these efforts, while desirable (albeit tardy), can achieve little more than a delay in the attainment of the ultimate teacher goal — a *bilateral* determination of these questions.

It is self-deluding to assume that teachers will be satisfied with half-measures on anything other than an interim basis. The greater gains of teachers in other states and local areas, produced by the greater militance of teacher organizations there, will have (indeed, *are* having) a disquieting effect. This means that the delaying potential of such measures will depend upon the extent to which school boards are willing unilaterally to accord their teachers substantially the same benefits as teachers are achieving elsewhere under a bilateral-determination format. In view of the political answerability of school board members to the voters who elect them and the difficulty politically of school fund-raising, it is reasonable to conclude that any continuation of unilateral determination of salaries, conditions of employment, and school policy will fall short of what teachers are able to achieve under a bilateral determination. Accordingly, a premium will be placed upon teacher militancy in the effort to achieve such benefits. School boards which refuse to accept this fact and which cling instead to their traditional "management prerogatives" will face not only the problems of recruitment and retention of personnel in an increasingly competitive market, but also the threat of rebellion by teachers too deeply rooted in the district to move elsewhere.

Again, as indicated in previous sections, the handwriting on school board walls is that of a changing of the guard in public education. The traditional unilateral determination of questions of strong consequence to teachers is passé. The approach of the California, Oregon, and Washington statutes, or similar palliatives, is not apt to get the job done on anything other than an interim basis, *unless* this approach is so liberally administered as to amount *in practice* to a bilateral determination of these questions. The latter is too much to expect.

Accordingly, the authors are of the view that realistic legislation should go beyond mere *consultation* and provide for actual *bilateral* determination of the questions of importance to public school teachers.

Should the statute indicate the scope or subject matter of negotiations? If so, what should the scope be?

There is a vast difference between that which is bargainable — i.e. properly a subject of bilateral determination — in private employment and in public education. In the former, the quite reasonable assumption is that there is a sphere of management prerogative into which the employees are not properly to be admitted. The private enterprise is run for profit; the entrepreneurs risk their capital to this end; the function of collective bargaining is to permit the employees to present their collective strength against the "boss" as a countervailing force against exploitation and oppression. A relatively narrow ambit therefore serves the purposes of collective bargaining in the private sector. Wages, hours, and conditions of employment, relatively narrowly defined, are the concern of the workers. If they are protected in these respects from the profit motive of the employer, any further protection is gratuitous — indeed, invasive of the competitive, risk-taking initiative that serves as the motive power of free enterprise. Accordingly, the nature, design, quality, and price of the product of the enterprise are properly relegated to unilateral management decision. Management is possessed of the essential expertise as to these matters. If its judgments are unsound, the business suffers the proper fate in the free enterprise scheme: it loses out to its competitors.

None of the foregoing is applicable to public education. Here, the purpose of the enterprise is not private profit, but sound education. The "entrepreneurs" — local school boards — are not engaged in competitive risk-taking for the sake of profit. Nor are they possessed of superior expertise in the pursuit of the product they function to produce. Quite the contrary, they are at best dilettantes as to what is, or is not, sound education. Conversely, their employees, the teachers, *are* trained *and* certified in the production and evaluation of sound education.

Accordingly, one may conclude that the public interest is best served by a more liberal view of that which is bargainable between teachers and school boards than is the case in private employment. In any event, this is decidedly the position of both the NEA and AFT, as reflected by

90

the pronouncements they make, the statutes they lobby for, and the contracts they negotiate. What is involved in their efforts is nothing short of a changed custodianship of public education.

Their case is most powerfully made, ironically, in two of the weakest existing teacher-negotiation statutes — those of California and Washington. The California statute provides that school employers "shall meet and confer" with employee representatives as to "all matters relating to employment conditions and employer-employee relations, including, but not limited to wages, hours and other terms and conditions of employment," and also as to "the definition of educational objectives, the determination of the content of courses and curricula, the selection of textbooks, and other aspects of the instructional program to the extent such matters are within the discretion of the public school employer or governing board under the law."[107] Similarly, the Washington statute provides that "representatives of an employee organization ... shall have the right ... to meet, confer and negotiate with the board ... or a committee thereof to communicate the considered professional judgment of the certificated staff prior to the final adoption by the board of proposed school policies relating to, but not limited to, curriculum, textbook selection, in-service training, student teaching programs, personnel, hiring and assignment practices, leaves of absence, salaries and salary schedules and noninstructional duties."[108]

The remaining statutes (Connecticut, Massachusetts, Michigan, Oregon, Rhode Island, and Wisconsin) confine the definition of bargainable issues, in somewhat varying language, to monetary compensation and conditions of employment. In focusing on what may be generically referred to as "conditions of employment," these statutes adopt the scope of bargaining as defined under the National Labor Relations Act for the private sector.[109] The elastic quality of this criterion has been amply demonstrated over the years of experience under the federal act; the scope of bargainable issues has gradually grown so as to encompass the new subjects rendered relevant by the evolution of the economy.

There is strong reason to believe, therefore, that this demonstrably elastic formula is an adequate guide for teacher bargaining. Almost no policy decision of a school board is without its effect upon the working conditions of teachers. As a consequence, there is room under the "con-

---

[107] *Cal. Educ. Code* secs. 13084 and 13085.

[108] *Rev. Code of Wash. Ann.* title 28 appendix 28.6 sec. 3.

[109] Labor-Management Relations Act, secs. 8(d) and 9(a), 61 Stat. 140, 143 (1947), 29 U.S.C. secs. 158(d) and 159(a) (1964).

ditions of employment" formula for teacher representatives to assert bargaining rights over such diverse matters as promotions, discipline procedures, transfers, class size, televised instruction, additions to the staff, extension of the school day or year, curriculum content, textbooks, allocation of money in the school budget. There is also room for school boards to contend that at least some of these matters are "not negotiable."

To the extent that the laws of the particular state dictate an answer to any of these matters (e.g. the number of days of instruction in a school year, tenure standards and procedures), the latter are, of course, removed from the bargaining table (and made the subject of lobbying). However, where the state law does not provide a specific answer, it is the judgment of the authors that almost all matters of sufficient concern to the teachers to warrant their arising during negotiations should be discussed at the bargaining table. This does not mean that school boards should relinquish the power of unilateral determination as to all such subjects broached by the teachers; it means rather that they should not adopt a "management rights" stance which precludes discussion, but should instead "demand" (i.e. bargain hard for) a retention of unilateral control over matters which, in their judgment, merit such. This approach by school boards would achieve four desirable ends. (1) It would preclude the bitterness and strife resulting from refusal even to discuss an issue on its merits. (2) It would require the board representatives to attempt to justify on a basis of reason their desire for maintaining unilateral control over the particular matter, thus rendering less tenable a position of "power for the sake of power." (3) It would expose the board to the potential enlightenment resulting from a full hearing of the teachers' views. (4) It would, reciprocally, expose the teachers to the potential enlightenment resulting from a full hearing of the board's views.

From an objective standpoint, it is difficult to see anything bad in the foregoing. School boards and administrators would, of course, lose the comfort of being able to take a position for no reason or for reasons they would prefer not to disclose. Teachers, on the other hand, would gain the satisfaction of joint exploration of subjects not specifically closed to discussion by state law. This gain by the teachers at the expense of the unilateral power of boards and administrators is, after all, what collective bargaining is all about. Unless it is concluded that professionally trained and duly certificated teachers have nothing to contribute to wiser educational policy, the only argument against admitting them to the process by which such policy is determined is the technical one of "sovereignty." The latter has been examined by the authors and found wanting in this application in the opening section of this chapter.

Accordingly, it is the view of the authors that a statute covering teacher bargaining should define the scope of bargaining, that the definition should certainly include salaries and other conditions of employment, and that the latter is a sufficiently encompassing and flexible formula to permit negotiations as to almost any question of educational policy not expressly preempted by state law. What resolution is to be made of these questions would thus be left to the process of bargaining accommodation in each local district, including, most specifically, the decision as to which issues are to be left to unilateral determination by the board.

Should the statute provide for a written agreement?

Five of the existing statutes provide for a reduction to writing of any agreement reached as a result of collective negotiations. Those of Massachusetts,[110] Rhode Island,[111] and Wisconsin[112] *require* such an agreement to be reduced to writing; those of Connecticut[113] and Michigan[114] require a writing "if requested by either party."

The Michigan and Wisconsin statutes have an interesting fillip: they permit the writing to be in the form of an ordinance or resolution of the public employer. This is to accord with the practice in some communities, antedating the statutes, of avoiding "delegation of power" (sovereignty) problems by substituting the ordinance or resolution procedure for that of a written contract as the final step in the process of collective agreement.

The Wisconsin statute has another interesting quirk: "Such agreements shall be binding on the parties only if express language to that effect is contained therein."[115]

The California, Oregon, and Washington statutes make no mention of written agreements. Indeed, none of them makes express mention of *agreements*, either oral *or* written.[116] What they grant, as previously

---

[110] *Ann. Laws of Mass.* ch. 149 sec. 1781.

[111] *Gen. Laws of R.I.* title 28 sec. 28–9. 3–4.

[112] *West's Wis. Stat. Ann.* ch. 111 sec. 111. 70(4) (i).

[113] *Conn. Gen. Stat. Ann.* title 10 sec. 10–153d.

[114] *Mich. Stat. Ann.* title 17 sec. 17. 455(15).

[115] n. 112 above.

[116] The Washington statute does contain an oblique reference in a section preserving "any lawful agreement heretofore entered" from abrogation by the act.

discussed, is *consultation* rights, although by implication they certainly seek to promote at least informal accords.

In the authors' view, a statute dealing with the negotiation rights of teachers should provide for the reduction of agreements reached to writing, at least where request for such is made by either party. This does not mean, of course, that the statute should require a written agreement or, indeed, any agreement at all; good faith effort to reach agreement is all that should be required. But where an agreement is in fact reached, the right of either party to demand that it be expressed in writing should be recognized.

The arguments in favor of this are obvious: a concrete and indisputable record exists of the terms of the agreement for reference in case of dispute. The only argument against the requirement of a writing is the one of "sovereignty": that the school board cannot delegate its power under state law of unilateral superintendence of school affairs. This argument reaches beyond objection to the reduction to writing of any agreement which is made; it attacks the power to make the agreement in *any* form.

The pros and cons of the sovereignty problem have been previously discussed. The only additional point we wish to make here is that the problem can, in any event, be squarely confronted in any written agreement by the express inclusion of a provision to the effect that any term of the agreement which is in conflict with state law shall be of no effect. This simply renders explicit what is implicit anyway and postpones for later judicial resolution the question of the legality of the contractual provisions in dispute — indeed, of the entire agreement if the sovereignty argument is pitched that profoundly. As a practical matter, the agreement is likely to be honored in any case, thus mooting any sovereignty arguments that might survive the enactment of the statute authorizing teacher bargaining. The process of voluntarily honoring the agreement will be greatly facilitated where it is reduced to writing.

Should the statute set the duration of the agreement and establish a "contract bar" precluding any challenge of the majority status of the teacher representative during the life of the contract?

The "contract bar" has already been preliminarily discussed in an earlier section.[117] Briefly restated, contract bar rules are the rules devel-

---

[117] See text at n. 76 above.

oped by the National Labor Relations Board which preclude the filing of a petition for a representation election during the life of an existing collective agreement, up to a maximum of three years. This means that once a collective agreement has been validly executed, it protects the incumbent employee representative from any challenge via a new election while the contract remains in effect or for a period of three years, whichever is shorter. The purpose of the contract bar is to bring stability to the bargaining relationship without unduly infringing upon the freedom of choice of bargaining representative by the employees involved. The latter consideration is what prompts the NLRB's current three-year limitation on the bar.

A few of the statutes presently authorizing collective negotiations by teachers have incorporated contract bar provisions. The Michigan statute is the most explicit:

> No election shall be directed in any bargaining unit . . . where there is in force and effect a valid collective bargaining agreement . . . which is of fixed duration: Provided, however, No collective bargaining agreement shall bar an election upon the petition of persons not parties thereto where more than 3 years have elapsed since the agreement's execution or last timely renewal, whichever was later.[118]

The Massachusetts statute likewise contains an express contract bar provision, but leaves the duration of the bar to administrative discretion: "No election shall be directed during the term of a collective bargaining agreement; except that for good cause shown the [state labor relations] commission may direct such an election."[119]

The Wisconsin statute is ambiguous. It provides that a collective agreement "may include a term for which it shall remain in effect not to exceed one year."[120] But the Wisconsin Employment Relations Board has held that such an agreement does not bar a new representation election, although if a new representative prevails in such election, it shall be bound by the provisions of the existing agreement.[121]

The Rhode Island statute is similarly ambiguous. It provides that no contract "shall exceed the term of three (3) years,"[122] but it also provides that "the state labor relations board upon the written petition for an election signed by not less than twenty percent (20%) of the

---

[118] *Mich. Stat. Ann.* title 17 sec. 17. 455(14).

[119] *Ann. Laws of Mass.* ch. 149 sec. 178H(3).

[120] *West's Wis. Stat. Ann.* ch. 111 sec. 111. 70(4) (i).

[121] The pertinent cases are discussed in *Section of Labor Relations Law — 1966, American Bar Association,* p. 178.

[122] *Gen. Laws of R.I.* title 28 sec. 28–9. 3–4.

certified public school teachers ... indicating their desire to change or withdraw recognition *shall forthwith* [but no more than once each twelve months] call and hold an election. ..."[123] It further provides that such election "must be held at least thirty (30) days before the expiration date of any employment contract."[124]

The remaining statutes authorizing teacher negotiations are completely silent on the contract bar question.

The view of the authors is that a teacher bargaining statute should, for the sake of stability, contain a contract bar provision. Their further view is that it should be of two years' duration. A lesser period is too short to allow the establishment of effective working relationships between the representative and the school board, particularly in view of the problem of budgetary deadlines, previously discussed.[125] A longer period is too invasive of the teachers' freedom of choice of representative, particularly in view of the "sweetheart" agreements that might ensue in school districts where the confrontation between the NEA and AFT has either not yet begun or not yet reached full proportions; the potential for resentment and strife would be increased by a longer-term bar in such situations.

V. Strikes, Sanctions, and Impasse Procedures

Should the strike be declared illegal? What of "sanctions," mass "resignations," withholding of "extracurricular" services, "working to rule"?

The real nub of the school teacher collective bargaining problem is not reached until it is asked: How are bargaining impasses to be resolved? In private employment the answer is by resort to economic coercion — i.e. strikes, lockouts, and the threat thereof. The right of private employees to strike and engage in concerted supportive activities such as picketing and boycotts is the motive power for agreement. The relative economic strength or staying power of the parties determines the content of the collective bargain.

The strike has rarely been considered legal in public employment.[126] At least fifteen states have enacted legislation specifically prohibiting

---

[123] *ibid.*, sec. 28–9. 3–5 (italics added).

[124] *ibid.*, sec. 28–9. 3–7.

[125] See pp. 78–79 above.

[126] For a discussion of teacher strikes, see Lieberman and Moskow, pp. 289–303. It is noted that "in Alberta, Saskatchewan, and Quebec, teachers have the right to strike by statute." *ibid.*, p. 301.

strikes by public employees.[127] In the absence of statutes, many state courts have applied sanctions, including the upholding of discharges of public employees, for strike activity.[128] Of the five state statutes mandating collective *bargaining,* as opposed to mere *consultation,* for teachers (Connecticut, Massachusetts, Michigan, Rhode Island, and Wisconsin), only that of Rhode Island does not expressly declare the strike illegal. The Rhode Island statute inversely declares that "nothing contained in this chapter shall be construed to accord to certified public school teachers the right to strike."[129] The California, Oregon, and Washington statutes, which grant only consultation rights, find no necessity to, and do not, mention strikes.[130]

The traditional view prohibiting strikes by public employees is usually justified on the basis of "sovereignty." Here, the sovereignty argument is at its strongest. It may be contended with considerable force that the mere execution of a collective bargaining contract by a school board, even though the contract be for a fixed term, does not constitute an unlawful delegation of the board's authority under law, but, on the contrary, is merely one way for the board to exercise its authority. This was, in fact, the holding of the Connecticut Supreme Court of Errors in *Norwalk Teachers' Association* v. *Board of Education,* discussed in the initial section of this chapter.[131] It is quite another matter, however, to take the next step and declare that it is also lawful for teachers to *coerce* the school board, by striking, to enter the kind of contract the teachers desire. Here, the school board cannot be said to be exercising its discretion via the collective agreement, since it is, to the extent of the coercion, not a free agent.

The Connecticut court drew precisely this distinction in the *Norwalk Teachers'* case. Regarding the strike, it said:

> In the American system, sovereignty is inherent in the people. They can delegate it to a government which they create and operate by law. They can give to that government the power and authority to perform certain duties and furnish certain services. The government so created and empowered must employ people to carry on its task. Those people are agents of the government. They exercise some part of the sovereignty entrusted to it. They occupy a status entirely different from

---

[127] The statutes are cited in Stinnett, pp. 32–33 n. 18.

[128] *ibid.,* pp. 33–34.

[129] *Gen. Laws of R.I.* title 28 sec. 28–9. 3–1.

[130] Oregon does, however, have another statute prohibiting "public employees" from striking. *Ore. Rev. Stat.* ch. 243 sec. 243.760.

[131] See text at n. 25 above.

those who carry on a private enterprise. They serve the public welfare and not a private purpose. To say that they can strike is the equivalent of saying that they can deny the authority of government and contravene the public welfare.[132]

As forceful as this argument is, it leaves school teacher and other public employee bargaining in a curious condition. The teachers may bargain collectively, but they may not engage in those demonstrations of strength which have generally been found necessary to produce meaningful agreement in such bargaining. They have, in short, the form without the substance.

This line of reasoning has produced a body of thought in support of legalizing teacher strikes. The strongest supporters of this point of view perceive a constitutional basis for their position. As stated by Moskow in his recent book, *Teachers and Unions*:

> Some authorities still maintain . . . that "no-strike" statutes are only constitutional when the health and safety of the public are endangered. They would have no objection to "no strike" legislation pertaining to policemen and firemen since this [sic] would clearly jeopardize the health and safety of the public. In private industry, the Taft-Hartley Act recognizes threats to health and safety *only* if a national emergency is created by the strike, and even then only a temporary injunction will be allowed. These authorities feel that statutes should at least say that under some circumstances public employees have the right to strike.[133]

Whatever may be said of the constitutional argument, little reason appears for denying the power of state legislatures to authorize strikes by school teachers and other public employees, at least where public health or safety is not thereby endangered. Indeed, the New Hampshire Supreme Court, in a 1957 case upholding the issuance of an injunction prohibiting a teacher organization from striking, had this to say: "There is no doubt that the Legislature is free to provide by statute that public employees may enforce their right to collective bargaining by arbitration or strike."[134]

A lower Minnesota court went even farther in a 1951 case when it said that to hold that a public employee has no right to strike simply because he is a public employee is

---

[132] Norwalk Teachers' Ass'n v. Board of Education, 83 A. 2d 482, 485 (Conn. 1951).

[133] Michael H. Moskow, *Teachers and Unions* (Philadelphia: University of Pennsylvania, the Wharton School of Finance and Commerce, Industrial Relations Department, 1966), Research Studies no. 42, p. 54.

[134] City of Manchester v. Manchester Teachers Guild, 131 A. 2d 59, 62 (N.H. 1957).

... to indulge in the expression of a personal belief and then ascribe to it a legality on some tenuous theory of sovereignty or supremacy of government. ... The right to strike is rooted in the freedom of man, and he may not be denied the right except by clear, unequivocal language embodied in a constitution, statute, ordinance, rule, or contract.[135]

Interestingly, the Minnesota legislature subsequently passed an antistrike act applicable to public employees.[136]

The AFT, with its labor orientation and affiliation, espouses the right of teachers to strike, carrying the espousal to the point of civil disobedience in the face of antistrike laws. The NEA, with its professional orientation, long eschewed the strike. But as its experience with collective bargaining (which it is increasingly willing to call by that name instead of "collective negotiations") has grown and as the confrontation with the AFT has become more intense, the NEA has undergone an interesting metamorphosis. It has moved from the idea of "sanctions" — in its most extreme form a kind of professional blacklisting of a school district, or entire state, for maintaining, in the NEA judgment, an unprofessional environment for teachers — to the weapons of mass "resignations," withholding of "extracurricular" services, "professional study days," and, finally, in some instances, to the spade-called-a-spade *strike*.

At this point it may be well to clarify the relationship, if any, between mass resignations, and the partial withholding of services, and antistrike laws. Are such teacher stratagems properly categorized as "strikes" under such laws, and therefore illegal, or are they not strikes, and therefore not reached by such legislation?

In dealing with this question, a closer look at the proscriptions in the teacher bargaining statutes is in order. The Connecticut statute prohibits "any strike or concerted refusal to render services."[137] The Massachusetts statute prohibits "any strike, work stoppage, slowdown or withholding of services."[138] The Wisconsin statute prohibits, simply, "strikes."[139]

---

[135] The case (involving a strike by school janitors) is quoted and discussed in Stinnett, p. 35. The decision of the lower court was affirmed by the Minnesota Supreme Court, without the necessity of comment upon the quoted passage, in Board of Education of City of Minneapolis v. Public School Employees' Union Local No. 63, 45 N.W. 2d 797 (Minn. 1951).

[136] *Minn. Stat. Ann.* ch. 179 secs. 179. 52–179. 57.

[137] *Conn. Gen. Stat. Ann.* title 10 sec. 10–153e.

[138] *Ann. Laws of Mass.* ch. 149 sec. 178M.

[139] *West's Wis. Stat. Ann.* ch. 111 sec. 111. 70(4) (1).

The definition in the Michigan statute is the most detailed: "the word 'strike' shall mean the concerted failure to report for duty, the wilful absence from one's position, the stoppage of work, or the abstinence in whole or in part from the full, faithful and proper performance of the duties of employment. . . ."[140]

Under any of these statutes, the partial withholding of services on a concerted basis would seem clearly unlawful. What this conduct amounts to is a partial strike — a strike "on the boss's time," and in that respect perhaps more reprehensible than a full strike because it places pressure on the employer without any offsetting loss of salary to the employees. Where the services withheld are "extracurricular," however, other problems enter. Such services include acting as faculty sponsor for student clubs (Science Club, Latin Club, Chess Club, Art Club, and the like), chaperoning school dances, participating in PTA work, etc. The question here is whether it is an express or implied term of the teacher's contract of employment that he render such after-hour services. If so, a concerted withholding of the services would constitute a partial strike. If not, the contrary would be the case. Since teachers' employment contracts are likely to be spare documents (if, indeed, there is any document at all), there is typically room for argument as to precisely what the teacher is being paid, and is therefore legally obligated, to do. "Working to rule," as the Canadians put it, can prove a most vexing pressure on school administrators, long accustomed to the performance by teachers, without question being raised, of a whole galaxy of twilight-zone services for which no *express* compensation or reciprocal obligation to perform exists.

The mass resignation of teachers, or, more accurately, the threat thereof, is another matter, raising questions somewhat unique in the employment relations field. Most school teachers, unlike public and private employees generally, are under *annual* contracts of employment. The term of each contract runs typically for the school year. The teacher is, in a sense, rehired for each new school year — i.e. his contract of employment is renewed. By way of contrast, most other employees, public and private, work not under contracts in the generally understood sense but, rather, under employments "at will." This means that neither such employees nor their employers commit themselves contractually as to future service or retention in service: the employee may quit *at will*, the employer may discharge *at will* (provided, of course, there is no collective bargaining agreement which restricts the employ-

---

[140] *Mich. Stat. Ann.* title 17 sec. 17. 455(1).

er's common-law rights). If the public employee is under civil service, the "at will" rights of his employer are, of course, circumscribed by the civil service regulations.

In view of the foregoing, the argument in favor of distinguishing mass resignations by teachers, or mass refusals to execute *new* employment contracts for the succeeding year, from the "strike" would run as follows: Teachers have no obligation, either individually or collectively, to enter new contracts of employment. Their only obligation is to honor the terms of the one-year contract under which they are currently employed. When the existing contract expires, they are free agents. Accordingly, they are free to engage in mass refusals to renew their contracts of employment.

There are, however, several flaws in this line of reasoning. In the first place, the existence of state tenure laws derogates from the "annual contract" view of teacher employment since such laws, in effect, assure continuance of employment from year to year, if the teacher so desires. Only the teacher is free to terminate the employment, not the school board. Similarly, the renewal of the teacher's contract is most perfunctorally accomplished, frequently by the mere passing of a specified date before which the teacher has not formally signified his intention to *resign*. What all of this boils down to is that teachers are employed under *annual* contracts in form only; in substance, their employment is continuous. The annual "contract renewal" is simply a vestige of an earlier era when there were no tenure laws, and when, as a consequence, there was in substance as well as form an annual reappraisal of the teacher–school board relationship and, where the reappraisal so warranted, a new contractual undertaking on each side for the ensuing year.

Moreover, while frequently *threatened* as a bargaining gambit, mass resignation of the teachers in a given school district has rarely, if ever, been carried out. Indeed, the credibility of the threat may be seriously questioned. It is quite something to believe that a substantial number of teachers in any given school district really intend to pull up roots, abandon the service credits they have earned (with consequent enhancement of their salaries), and seek teaching employment elsewhere or abandon the profession altogether. And the greater the number threatening to do so, the less credible the threat because the likelihood of their being absorbed in neighboring school districts, so as not to have to give up their present homes, would be decreased.

What the threat of mass resignation amounts to, therefore, is a sophisticated technique for bringing pressure to bear on a school board. If the school board resists the pressure of the threat, the implementation of the threat will almost surely consist of the teachers sitting back during the course of the summer and awaiting the reopening of the schools in the fall, confident that in the present sellers' market for teacher services, and in the face of the "professional sanctions" (blacklisting) surely to be invoked against the school district, the board will not be able to obtain anywhere near the necessary number of replacements. If the bargaining impasse is not resolved by the time school reopens, the mass resignation becomes in effect a strike. Public pressure on the school board increases to the point where concessions are made, and the teachers then return to work under a settlement agreement requiring the taking back of *all* those who had "resigned."

Full analysis of the mass-resignation device thus reveals it to be a concerted effort to pressure the school board into granting concessions in conditions of employment through the withholding of services — *ergo,* a "strike." The strong likelihood is that it will be so treated in the interpretation of antistrike legislation.

There are, however, two differences between this device and the standard strike which bear noting. The first is that the device is less flexible and more cumbersome from the teachers' standpoint than the strike. The ultimate pressure of the device is postponed until the reopening of the schools, which means that this kind of "strike" must always occur in September, a poor timing in view of the budgetary deadlines of the prior spring and summer. Moreover, the delay in impact between the announcement of the threat and the actual work stoppage, conjoined with the questionable credibility of the threat, makes it a much less potent weapon at the bargaining table.

The second difference is that the mass-resignation device, because of its relative sophistication, is not as patently violative of antistrike laws. To this extent, it may present a better image of the profession to the public.

Interesting as all this is, the authors expect the present trend of both the AFT and NEA to continue. The former endorses the strike, however illegal, as a necessary exercise in civil disobedience in the face of a bad (antistrike) law. The latter, with some embarrassment, feels itself driven to the same conclusion, as much by what it is currently learning about the nature of collective bargaining as by the need to match the AFT in militancy in the competition for teacher allegiance. The out-and-out strike, legal or illegal, is thus the bargaining-pressure technique which teachers may be expected increasingly to rely upon in the immediate future.

We are, as a consequence, squarely confronted with the question of whether a teacher bargaining statute *should* outlaw the strike. The question underlying this is whether such a law would have any effect other than to render strikes illegal; would it, in fact, cut down on the *incidence* of teacher strikes? It is difficult, if not impossible, to answer this question in any generalized manner at present. One fact, at least, is clear: there have probably been more teacher strikes and threats of strikes in the last couple of years, most, if not all, of them illegal, than we have experienced in any comparable period of our history. They have been centered, as one would expect, in large metropolitan areas — both urban and suburban — where industrialism and unionism are well advanced.

The experience in Michigan is instructive. The Public Employment Relations Act went into effect on July 23, 1965. While authorizing collective bargaining by school teachers and other public employees, it continued the ban on their striking which had long been in effect in Michigan. During the first year of operation under the new statute, there were eleven strikes, all of them against school boards. Nine of these were teacher strikes. Interestingly, while five were called by AFT affiliates, four were called by NEA affiliates (some labelled "professional study days").[141] All of these resulted in collective bargaining agreements of substantial benefit to the teachers involved. Most were resolved after only a few days of strike; the longest strike entailed a loss of two weeks of school. In other Michigan districts, contracts were successfully negotiated without resort to strikes, in no small part, we may conclude, because the credibility of strike *threats* (spoken and unspoken) had been established elsewhere.

The Michigan experience suggests that the express statutory recognition of the right of teachers to bargain collectively carries with it the likelihood of increased strike activity, even though the latter be declared illegal. But the current militancy of teachers and other public employees is not the product of recognition of bargaining rights any more than civil rights militancy is the product of civil rights laws. Teacher strikes have occurred and been threatened in state after state having no law authorizing teacher bargaining. The militancy manifested in these strikes and threatened strikes is the product of the postwar lag of public employees behind private employees with respect to employment benefits, including the right of some voice in the determination of conditions of employment. The situation in public employment now is akin to the

---

141 Robert G. Howlett, "Resolution of Impasses in Employee Relations in Public Education," a paper presented at the conference described in n. 47 above.

situation in private employment in the late thirties, after passage of the Wagner Act.

The answer of a free society to the problem of teacher strikes is not, therefore, to suppress teacher bargaining any more than the answer to private-sector strikes is to repeal the National Labor Relations Act. Change is the law of life and must be adjusted to institutionally. What we need are techniques for resolving teacher bargaining impasses which will minimize strikes. Merely outlawing strikes is not enough, because, as we have seen, this does not prevent strikes, but only renders them illegal. And if we are to have strikes by teachers *anyway*, there is strong argument for legalizing them in order to maintain respect for law — particularly in the case of teachers since they are apt to serve as models for their students, either in keeping or breaking the law.

Accordingly, the view of the authors is as follows: (1) Collective bargaining by teachers is desirable. (2) Strikes by teachers are not desirable. (3) Antistrike legislation is extremely difficult of enforcement absent substitute impasse-resolving techniques. (4) Such impasse-resolving techniques are themselves most difficult of effective application, for reasons to be developed in a subsequent section. (5) The most effective impasse-resolving technique, short of legalizing the strike, is binding arbitration. (6) The argument against binding arbitration — namely, that it kills collective bargaining because the parties will merely go through the forms of bargaining in the interest of jockeying for position before the ultimate arbitration board — while applicable in the private sector where the alternative motive power of the strike toward settlement is available, is not applicable in the public sector where strikes are illegal. (7) If we are serious about making teacher strikes illegal, we must provide an effective alternative to the strike, both from the standpoint of fairness and of enforceability of the antistrike measures. (8) Enforceability of antistrike laws will be considerably enhanced where the teachers strike in the teeth of an arbitration award binding upon the school board, since public opinion will not be as likely to support the teachers' cause.

The authors will have more to say as to the structuring of the binding-arbitration alternative to the strike in a subsequent section. For present purposes, it is necessary only to add that a simple legalizing of the strike by public employees is ill-conceived, in their judgment, for the following reasons: (1) There is a ceiling upon what employees in the private sector can demand and seek to obtain via the strike, imposed by the potential of bankrupting the employer. No such ceiling exists in public employment, where the public employer is in a monopoly position and obligated under law to maintain the service. (2) The function of the public employee strike is not the same as that of a strike by private employees. In the private sector, the strike seeks, most basically, to determine an equitable division of the profits of the enterprise between labor and capital. In the public sector, the strike seeks to bring pressure to bear not primarily upon the public employer — e.g. the school board — but rather upon the public whose interests the striking employees serve. The school board members, in the case of a teacher strike, are middlemen, conduits, through whom the teachers seek to bring pressure upon the public in order to stimulate a willingness on the part of the latter to bear the burden of higher taxes or new bond issues. The latter is a pressure from which the public should be free. Any pressure on the public to this end should be a *political* pressure rather than an *economic* pressure. The former allows for the free play of the political forces and techniques of a free society. The latter smacks of a kind of extortion or blackmail.

Under only one set of circumstances would the authors see fit to legalize a teacher strike. That is where the *school board* refuses to honor an arbitration award resolving an impasse in bargaining. The statute creating the impasse-resolving procedures via arbitration might specifically provide that the teachers are to be bound by the arbitration award if, *but only if,* the school board itself accepts the award; if the board refuses to comply with the award, the teachers would be free to engage in a legal strike. Such a scheme would allow a school board some leeway to resist the arbitration award (in contrast to completely binding arbitration) where it was deemed to be sufficiently out of keeping with the public interest, as conceived by the board members, to warrant resistance, and at the same time would allow the teachers to "take the issue to the public" via a strike, if in their view the issue so merited. Strikes in the teeth of the award would remain illegal, and the likelihood of rallying the kind of public opinion necessary to enforce the statutory sanctions against such a strike would be maximized, in sharp contrast to the antienforcement environment likely to exist where *all* teacher strikes are deemed illegal. Donald H. Wollett has espoused this plan as an answer to impasse-resolving in the teacher area.[142] The authors see much merit in it.

---

[142] n. 47 above.

If the strike is to be declared illegal, what penalties should be imposed? Against individuals? Against employee organizations?

The enforcement of antistrike laws is a difficult enterprise, as experience demonstrates. Basically, there are four types of sanctions that may be brought to bear: (1) The injunctive power of the courts. This has the virtue of flexibility, inherent in the discretionary power of the court. If the court's injunction is violated, it may impose penalties, including imprisonment of individuals and fines upon individuals and/or organizations, for contempt of its order. (2) The imposition of penalties by the employer for misconduct, including reprimand, fine, loss of benefits, demotion, suspension, and dismissal. (3) The denial or revocation of recognition of the employee organization. (4) The imposition of criminal penalties via the courts. The federal government, for example, requires all employees to sign sworn statements to the effect that they do not belong to "an organization of government employees" asserting the right to strike against the government and that they will not participate in any such strike. Violation is made a felony.[143]

Most of the statutes authorizing teacher bargaining which outlaw the strike do not address the problem of sanctions. An exception is that of Michigan, which speaks in terms of employee discipline or discharge and provides for judicial review at the instance of the offending employee.[144] The deficiencies of the Michigan statute as to sanctions are made ludicrously clear by a recent decision of a Michigan court denying an injunction against a teacher strike in Flint on the ground that the statutorily imposed sanction of employee discipline is exclusive of all others, including the injunction (as to which the statute is silent).[145]

Even more ludicrous has been the experience under the ill-famed Condon-Wadlin Act of New York,[146] which deals only in the negative with public employment disputes, proscribing strikes and prescribing severe and automatic penalties with surgical precision. Under Condon-Wadlin, the transit workers who struck in January of 1966 could not, for example, receive a wage increase for three years, despite the fact that the strike had been finally settled on the basis of a substantial

---

[143] 69 Sta. 624–625 (1955), 5 U.S.C. secs. 118p–118r.

[144] *Mich. Stat. Ann.* title 17 sec. 17. 455(6).

[145] Board of Education of the City of Flint, File No. 7375, Genesee County, June 1, 1966, reported in BNA Government Employee Relations Report, No. 145, June 20, 1966, p. B-1.

[146] N.Y. Civ. Serv. Law sec. 108.

wage increase. When a taxpayer's suit[147] presaged the only order the trial court could render under the law — an injunction against the payment of the increase — frantic efforts on the part of the New York legislature became necessary to prevent a second strike; the transit workers were hastily granted a legislative exemption from the law.[148]

This Condon-Wadlin fiasco resulted in the appointment by Governor Rockefeller of a committee of outstanding labor relations experts, under the chairmanship of Professor George W. Taylor. The report of this committee and the bill it proposed (popularly known as the "Taylor Report" and the "Taylor Bill") reflect the most sophisticated study yet made of antistrike law sanctions.

The sanctions recommended by the "Taylor Bill"[149] are as follows:

(1) Public employees who strike are "subject to the disciplinary penalties provided by law for misconduct," these being reprimand, fine, demotion, suspension, or dismissal, depending on the extent of the misconduct.[150] (In the case of teachers it could entail loss of certification.[151])

(2) An employee organization which instigates a strike is subject to loss of its right of recognition as representative of public employees, either indefinitely or for a specified period of time. In determining the guilt of the employee organization, one of the factors to be considered is whether the public employer "engaged in such acts of extreme provocation as to detract from the responsibility of the employee organization for the strike."[152]

(3) "... [W]here it appears that public employees or an employee organization threaten or are about to [strike] ... the chief legal officer of the government involved shall forthwith apply to the supreme court for an injunction against such violation. If an order of the court enjoining or restraining such violation does not receive compliance, such chief legal officer shall forthwith apply to the supreme court to punish

---

[147] Weinstein v. New York City Transit Authority, 49 Misc. 2d 170, 267 N.Y.S. 2d 111 (Sup. Ct. Feb. 9, 1966).

[148] Ch. 6, 1966 Laws of N.Y., Feb. 16, 1966.

[149] S. Int. No. 4784, Pr. No. 5689 (1966).

[150] ibid., sec. 2, art. 14 210(2).

[151] See the order of censure issued by James E. Allen, Jr., Commissioner of Education of the State of New York, on March 28, 1966, against the teachers who struck earlier that month in Plainview, L.I. The matter is discussed in Section of Labor Relations Law — 1966, American Bar Association, p. 171.

[152] S. Int. No. 4784, Pr. No. 5689 (1966), sec. 210(3).

such violation. . . ."[153] Punishment for a contempt may be by imprisonment and/or by fine "in an amount fixed in the discretion of the court."[154]

Some important differences between the sanctions proposed in the Taylor Bill and those provided in Condon-Wadlin are these: (1) The Taylor Bill operates to deprive employee organizations of recognition and representation rights which are otherwise extended to them by the bill. (2) The Taylor Bill *requires* the public employer to seek an injunction against a threatened strike. (3) The penalties under the Taylor Bill are not automatic; discretion is available to make the punishment fit the offense.

But the overriding difference between the Taylor Bill and Condon-Wadlin is that the former expressly accords collective bargaining rights to public employees (including teachers) and also provides impasse-resolving procedures in place of the prohibited strikes. The real thrust of the Taylor Bill is to render strikes by public employees *unnecessary,* not merely unlawful. The likelihood of achieving this most desirable but illusive goal is considered in the next section.

What impasse-breaking procedures should be developed?

The real dilemma of collective bargaining in public employment, as we have seen, is the absence of any effective means or incentive for the parties to avoid a stalemate. The employees cannot strike, and therefore should not threaten to strike. The employer cannot lock out. The parties can, of course, continue to talk, to reason, but it may be accepted as axiomatic that each side considers its position reasonable and the other's unreasonable. Moreover, the budgetary deadline looms nearer and nearer.

Obviously, outsiders must be brought in as catalysts or arbiters. The full panoply of uses to which these outsiders may be put is as follows: (1) mediation; (2) fact finding; (3) non-binding recommendations for settlement (advisory arbitration); (4) binding recommendations (binding arbitration).

All of the eight statutes prescribing teacher negotiations provide some impasse-resolving procedures through the use of outsiders, with the sole exception of California. While the language of the statutes is not always explicit as to the precise function and powers of the outsiders, a fair reading indicates that mediation, fact finding, and non-binding recom-

[153] *ibid.,* sec. 211.

[154] *ibid.,* sec. 3, amending sec. 751 of the Judiciary Law.

mendations are available under all seven. The Rhode Island statute is the only one of these which takes the next and final step of binding arbitration, but the range of issues subjected to binding arbitration is narrow. The Rhode Island statute reads: "The decision of the arbitrators shall be made public and shall be binding upon the certified public school teachers and their representative and the school committee on all matters not involving the expenditure of money."[155]

The reluctance to subject the resolution of bargaining impasses to binding arbitration, the most obvious substitute for the strike from a lay standpoint, is the product of two fears. The first is the old bugaboo of sovereignty. The second is the concern that this would destroy collective bargaining.

The sovereignty argument we have already explored elsewhere. In the immediate context, it consists of the idea that the superintendence of school affairs is entrusted under the law to school boards, and that this power cannot be delegated to a board of arbitrators. In the words of the Taylor Report to Governor Rockefeller: "Compulsory arbitration is not recommended. There is serious doubt whether it would be legal because of the obligation of the designated executive heads of government departments or agencies not to delegate certain fiscal and other duties."[156] Curiously, however, the Taylor Report immediately adds: "Voluntary arbitration on an ad hoc basis is a desirable course, on the other hand, *although it also leads to binding decisions*."[157] The Report argues strenuously the wisdom of a *contractual* commitment by the public employer and the employee representative to submit a dispute over wages and other conditions of employment to "arbitration" or to "fact-finding with recommendations, with or without the advance commitment by one or both parties to accept the recommendations. The procedures may provide a number of variants. The negotiators may jointly agree in advance to accept the recommendations of the fact-finders and to urge their acceptance upon their principals. They may jointly agree in advance to take the recommendations to the appropriate legislative body to advocate jointly the requisite appropriation or change in regulations, recognizing the authority of such legislative body."[158]

The wisdom of impasse-resolution contractually agreed upon is clear, and legislation encouraging it is strongly to be commended. But, on the

---

[155] *Gen. Laws of R.I.* title 28 sec. 28–9. 3–12.

[156] *Governor's Committee on Public Employee Relations, Final Report,* March 31, 1966, p. 46.

[157] *ibid.* (italics added).

[158] *ibid.*, pp. 35–36.

sovereignty front, what magic is there in distinguishing between legislative *permission* being given to public employers to contract in advance for binding arbitration of bargaining disputes and a legislative *mandate* that such impasses be resolved by binding arbitration *whether or not there has been any prior voluntary contractual commitment to that effect?* Is it the point of the Taylor Report that while the public employer may *itself* delegate its "fiscal and other duties," the legislature may not do the delegating for it? If so, this is a curious position, at least in the case of school boards, since the latter are creatures of the legislature and have only the powers legislatively bestowed upon them. If the legislature can give a school board the power unilaterally to determine conditions of employment and the power to contract away this power to an arbitrator, why cannot the legislature bestow the power of such determination, in the case of an impasse, *directly* upon an arbitrator or board of arbitrators, or, indeed, upon a "fact finder"?

It is not necessary to belabor this legal question, however, because a closer reading of the Report makes it clear that the real concern of the Taylor Committee is that compulsory (i.e. legislatively directed) arbitration is incompatible with collective bargaining. The Report states:

> The Committee has rejected the proposal for compulsory arbitration not merely because there may be serious questions as to its legality but because of the conviction that impasse disputes may arise less frequently and be settled more equitably by the procedures outlined in this report. In our judgment, the requirement for binding arbitration would likely reduce the prospects of settlement at earlier stages closer to the problems, the employees and the agency; it would tend to frustrate the participation of employees in the determination of compensation and conditions of employment and tend to encourage arbitrary and extreme positions on both sides.[159]

This is an admirable statement of the classic view of the effect of compulsory arbitration in the area of private employment, where collective bargaining is, at base, a test of economic strength, the weapons of strike and lockout hovering over the bargaining table. But does it follow that the same is true in public employment, where these weapons, the Taylor Report agrees, should not be available? Our guess is that, as applied to school teachers in a district where NEA and AFT affiliates are in strong competition, the school board and teacher representative are going to bargain to impasse, conservatively stated, more often than not, largely over money issues. If they have seen fit to agree upon im-

---

[159] *ibid.*, pp. 37–38.

passe procedures entailing more than mere mediation, the likelihood may be strong that the recommendations resulting, binding or not, will be honored. The reason for this is that these procedures, being the product of mutual agreement, carry with them an implied, if not express, obligation of good-faith observance by the parties. This is, of course, the strength of contractually created impasse procedures.

But what if the parties do not so agree? If the school board is jealous of its prerogatives, as many are, why should it so agree? Theoretically, it has no strike to fear. Why should it place itself under even an *implied* obligation of good-faith adherence to an arbitrator's award or a fact-finder's recommendations? And if the teacher representative is an AFT affiliate, sold on the righteousness of the strike, legal or illegal, why should it commit itself in any way to arbitration or fact finding with recommendations? To so do would be to derogate from the righteousness of its strike threat, however unspoken the latter may be. Indeed, if the teacher representative is an NEA affiliate and therefore, at best, a reluctant convert to the cause of teacher strikes, why should it prejudice itself in the continuing competition with the AFT by restricting in any degree its freedom of action? The willingness of an NEA affiliate to make this concession where the right of collective bargaining is bestowed upon it by the grace of a progressive school board (as happened in Rochester, New York[160]) is hardly demonstrative of a similar willingness where the right is a product of state law, as would be the case under the Taylor Bill. Perhaps we are unduly Machiavellian, but we are not as sanguine as the Taylor Committee about contractually based impasse resolution in the teacher area.

We must turn, therefore, to an examination of the Taylor Bill's non-contractual — i.e. statutory — impasse procedures. These are: (1) Mediation under the guidance of the Public Employment Relations Board, which the bill would create. (2) Appointment of a fact-finding board by the PERB to consist of "not more than three members, each representative of the public, from a list of qualified persons maintained by the board, which fact-finding board shall have . . . the power to make public recommendations for the resolution of the dispute."[161] (3) Further recommendations by the PERB. (4) A submission by "the chief executive officer of the government involved [chairman of the school board?]" of the fact-finding board's findings of fact and recommendations "to the

---

[160] See *Section of Labor Relations Law — 1966, American Bar Association*, pp. 168–169.

[161] S. Int. No. 4784, Pr. No. 5689 (1966), sec. 209(3) (b).

legislative body of the government involved [school board?]," "together with his recommendations for settling the dispute; and the employee organization may submit to such legislative body its recommendations for settling the dispute."[162]

Whatever may be said of the first three steps, the fourth leaves considerable to be desired as applied to school teacher bargaining. Ostensibly, it leaves to the school board the final resolution of the bargaining dispute between that school board and the teachers it employs! It would seem that the Taylor Committee did not have *independent* school districts in mind when it framed these procedures, despite the fact that these outnumber the half-dozen dependent districts in the State of New York many times over. But the six dependent school districts do include the most populous cities of the state, and in these the "legislative body of the government involved" would apparently be the city council. In such districts, the Taylor Bill provisions would, in effect, result in a kind of state-legislature mandated "binding arbitration" by the city council. This, too, leaves something to be desired, however, from the standpoint of the teachers, since on the core money issues the city council's niggardliness, as viewed by the teachers, is apt to be what produced the bargaining impasse in the first place — the dependent school board being a captive ultimately of the council's budget. One may be forgiven a little pessimism as to whether such a procedure is well calculated to stave off strikes.

Preferable in the view of the authors would be a scheme which provided the teachers with the lawful right to strike if, but only if, the recommendations of the fact-finding body appointed by the PERB were not honored by the purse-controlling authority, be it an independent school district or, where dependent, the city council. This alternative seems preferable to completely binding arbitration since it provides an escape for the school board where the fact finders are deemed by it to have gone "haywire." The public interest, as viewed by the school board, would be protected to this extent. Conversely, the refusal of the school board to accept the recommendations would trigger the offsetting rights of the teachers to strike. If this were the law, there might be more likelihood of the parties contractually committing themselves to arbitration of the bargaining dispute because of the greater control this would give them over the constituency of the impasse-resolving body. Moreover, teachers would be less likely to strike illegally under such a scheme — i.e. in defiance of the fact-finders' recommendations — and if

---

[162] *ibid.,* sec. 209(3) (e).

they did so strike, the climate of public opinion would be the best possible for enforcement of the statutory sanctions against such a strike.

VI. Administering Agency

By what agency should a teacher bargaining statute be administered?

There are at least six arrangements possible for the administering of teacher bargaining, which includes the problems of unit determination, conduct of representation elections, disposition of unfair practice charges, and the resolution of bargaining impasses.

The first is to place these matters under the jurisdiction of the state labor board, the body which administers collective bargaining in the private sector. This is the approach favored by the AFT and, indeed, adopted under the Massachusetts, Michigan, and Wisconsin statutes. It usually entails, as in the latter three states, a statutory lumping of teachers in with other public employees. On the other hand, the Rhode Island statute, dealing solely with school teachers, also places the responsibility for administering the representation and unfair practice phases of the statute in the hands of the state labor board. The statute, however, leaves the impasse-resolving procedures to the discretion of the parties. Either of them "may request mediation and conciliation upon any and all unresolved issues by the state department of education, the director of labor or from any other source."[163] Similarly, either party may request arbitration of unresolved issues "by sending such request by certified mail ... to the other party, setting forth the issues to be arbitrated."[164] Thereafter, the teacher representative and school board each name one arbitrator, and these two select a third who acts as chairman. In the alternative, the teacher representative and school board may agree to have the state board of education designate the arbitrator or arbitrators.

The second arrangement is to place the administration of teacher bargaining under the state education department. This is the approach favored by the NEA. None of the existing statutes employs this technique in pure form, although that of Connecticut does entrust certain administrative duties to the "secretary of the state board of education." Under this statute petitions for representation elections are filed with him, and he in turn notifies the local school board involved of the fact of filing. Similarly, in the event of an impasse in bargaining, "the disagreement

---

[163] *Gen. Laws of R.I.* title 28 sec. 28–9. 3–9.
[164] *ibid.*

shall be submitted to the secretary of the state board of education for mediation. The parties shall meet with him or his agents and provide such information as he may require. The secretary may recommend a basis for settlement but such recommendations shall not be binding upon the parties."[165] This is the extent of the involvement of the state board of education in the administration of the Connecticut statute. However, the secretary of the state board has issued some "Suggestions for Operating under P.A. No. 298," clarifying certain procedures where the statute is either silent or ambiguous.[166]

A third arrangement for the administration of teacher bargaining is to leave such issues as arise thereunder to *ad hoc* determination and management. This is the technique most centrally employed under the Connecticut statute, the product of a lobbying compromise between the NEA and AFT. All of the vital procedures under that statute are left to the administration of impartial persons or organizations mutually agreed upon by the teacher representatives and school boards. Thus, representation elections are conducted by "an impartial person or agency" mutually selected.[167] In practice, this has most often been the American Arbitration Association, which has a special election division for handling such matters. Disputes as to the agency to conduct the election or as to the eligibility of personnel to vote "shall be submitted to a board of arbitration" consisting of one representative chosen by each competing teacher organization, on the one hand, and an equal number of representatives chosen by the school board, on the other, these in turn selecting an "additional impartial member."[168] In practice, disputes as to time, place, and manner of elections and eligibility of voters have been resolved by an "election moderator," jointly selected by the competing teacher organizations and the school board, who then performs his function in cooperation with the AAA representatives responsible for the actual conducting of the election.[169] Bargaining impasses which cannot be resolved through the mediation efforts of the secretary of the state board of education are submitted to *ad hoc* tripartite advisory arbitration, the teacher representative selecting one member of the arbitration board, the school board another, and the two thus chosen selecting a third. "If the parties are unable to agree upon a third arbitrator, either

---

[165] *Conn. Gen. Stat. Ann.* title 10 sec. 10–153f(a).

[166] See n. 63 above.

[167] *Conn. Gen. Stat. Ann.* title 10 sec. 10–153b(b).

[168] *ibid.*, sec. 10–153c.

[169] The Hartford experience, a prototype, is described in *Section of Labor Relations Law — 1966, American Bar Association*, pp. 159–160.

party may petition the superior court . . . to designate the third arbitrator. . . ."[170]

A fourth method for administering teacher bargaining is exemplified by the Taylor Bill in New York. This bill would create an independent state agency, the Public Employment Relations Board, to administer all public employee bargaining. Incorporated in the bill, however, is a desirable flexibility permitting the creation of local procedures by county and municipal employers, including local school districts, "to resolve disputes concerning the representation status of employee organizations of employees of such government," including questions of unit determination and the conduct of elections.[171] Similarly, as we have seen, the bill authorizes contractual agreements between public employers and employee representatives for the resolution of bargaining impasses.

A fifth method of administering teacher bargaining would entail the creation of an independent agency which, unlike the Public Employment Relations Board of the Taylor Bill, would be restricted in its jurisdiction to school teacher matters.

A sixth method is to entrust administration to local school boards. This approach is adopted by the Oregon statute, which states that "the district school board shall establish election procedures and shall certify the [teachers'] committee which has been elected by the certificated school personnel. . . ."[172] However, the Oregon statute provides for advisory *ad hoc* arbitration of any "persistent disagreement over a matter of salaries or economic policies affecting professional services" by a board of "consultants," one of whom is selected by the school board, one by the teachers, and the third chosen by the other two members.[173] The California statute directs that the "public school employer shall adopt reasonable rules and regulations for the administration of employer-employee relations under this article" and, with respect to representation questions, "shall include provision for verifying the number of certificated employees of the public school employer who are members in good standing of an employee organization" for the purpose of determining the proportion of representation properly to be allocated to each teacher organization under the proportional representation scheme of the California statute.[174] However, "each employee organization shall adopt procedures for selecting its proportionate share of members of the nego-

[170] *Conn. Gen. Stat. Ann.* title 10 sec. 10–153f(b).
[171] S. Int. No. 4784, Pr. No. 5689 (1966), secs. 206 and 207.
[172] *Ore. Rev. Stat.* ch. 342 sec. 342. 460(2).
[173] *ibid.*, sec. 342. 470.
[174] *Cal. Educ. Code* sec. 13087.

tiating council. . . ."[175] The Washington statute, while less express with respect to the administration of representation matters, contains the same language as the California statute regarding the adoption by school boards of "reasonable rules and regulations for the administration of employer-employee relations under this act."[176] On the other hand, disputes in the negotiations authorized by the act are, upon the request of either the employee organization or the school board, presented for "assistance and advice" to a "committee composed of educators and school directors appointed by the state superintendent of public instruction."[177]

In evaluating the foregoing patterns of administration, it is easier to eliminate the undesirable arrangements than to recommend the desirable. The state labor board and state department of education alternatives are both objectionable on the obvious grounds that the first favors the AFT philosophy of teacher bargaining and the second favors that of the NEA. Neither of these philosophies contains sufficient wisdom unto itself to be accepted whole-hog, quite apart from the prejudice to one organization or the other from the adoption of either; a wiser course is some accommodation between the two. The alternative of local school board administration is objectionable to both organizations and to objective evaluation since it places critical control in the *employer*.

The authors are of the view that the best administrative resolution is through reliance on *ad hoc* procedures, mutually agreed upon by the parties, with either a Public Employment Relations Board, *à la* the Taylor Bill, in the background to deal with matters upon which no agreement can be reached, or an independent agency restricted in its jurisdiction to the administration of school teacher bargaining. As between these two, the argument in favor of the PERB approach is that it is more economical because it covers the entire field of public employment and therefore entails less redundancy of administrative effort. The argument in favor of a completely separate administration for school teacher matters is that this would ensure the most sophisticated handling of teacher bargaining, which because of the professional aspect of teaching and the crucial importance of education in a democratic society presents unique problems.

On balance, the authors favor the latter approach. In practice, the likelihood under the former of a differential treatment of school teach-

---

[175] *ibid.,* sec. 13085.
[176] *Rev. Code of Wash. Ann.* title 28 appendix 28. 6 sec. 8.
[177] *ibid.,* sec. 6.

ers, in recognition of the many distinct problems of public education as compared to other less-sensitive areas of public enterprise, does not seem very strong. What seems more likely to occur is a blurring of the differences in the process of administration, a result already discernible, for example, under the generic administrative design of the Michigan statute where the Michigan Labor Mediation Board has tried and largely abandoned the effort to provide specialized personnel for the administration of school teacher bargaining. The authors fear the effect upon public education of the lack of sophisticated administration of collective bargaining in such employment — a lack which is potential, if not indeed inherent, in any scheme which tends to equate teachers with, for example, trash collectors.

VII. Summary of Recommendations

In view of the length of the foregoing discussion of questions involved in teacher-bargaining legislation, it may be useful to summarize very briefly the major recommendations made. Readers who have valiantly negotiated the chapter to this point may find in this a convenient check list of the major conclusions of the authors concerning such legislation. Those who routinely confine their reading to conclusions and summaries may find themselves sufficiently provoked or intrigued to thumb back through the chapter and sample its smörgåsbord.

Boldly and baldly stated, the conclusions are these:

There is need for legislation concerning the collective bargaining rights of public school teachers. Such legislation should single teachers out for separate treatment, rather than lumping them in with other public employees. The statute should provide flexibility of bargaining-unit determination, allowing local option as to whether supervisory and administrative personnel should be included in the same unit with classroom teachers. The determination of teacher representatives should be by secret ballot. The organization selected by a majority of the teachers voting should be granted exclusive bargaining rights for all those employed in the unit. The right of exclusive representation should last for two years; representation elections should be held not more than once every two years.

The legislation should make it unlawful for a school board or administrator to discriminate against employees on the basis of membership or non-membership in an employee organization, or otherwise to interfere with organizational activities. It should also require both the school board and the teacher representative to bargain in good faith. The scope or subject matter of teacher–school board negotiations should be broad enough to encompass not only salaries, hours, and working conditions in the narrow sense, but also questions of educational policy. As to this subject matter, bilateral determination, not mere consultation, should be required, leaving it open, of course, for school boards to "bargain hard" for unilateral control over any matter deemed to merit such control. Any agreement reached should be required to be reduced to writing, upon request.

The strike should be declared illegal, and impasse-resolving procedures provided, including the final step of arbitration or fact finding with recommendations; however, in the event the school board refuses to abide by the decision of the arbitration body or the recommendations of the fact finders, the teachers should then have the right to strike.

The statute should allow the parties to agree upon their own agencies for the administration of teacher bargaining, including the resolution of representation disputes, unit determinations, conduct of elections, and procedures for resolving bargaining impasses, with an independent state agency in the background to deal with matters upon which no agreement can be reached. This independent agency should be restricted in its jurisdiction to the administration of teacher bargaining.

IV

Implications of Collective Bargaining for the Quality of Education: A Look Ahead

THAT THE MOVEMENT TOWARD FOR-malizing the employment relationship in public education will gain force in the years ahead seems clear. The unsatisfactory employment conditions discussed in the first chapter of this volume will not go away by themselves, and the frustrations caused by these conditions will prompt greater numbers of teachers to seek some form of bilateral determination of the employment arrangement. Competition between the two major teacher organizations has by no means run its course; it will itself continue to generate a considerable amount of organizational activity. And as we saw in the previous chapter, legislation designed to accommodate the desire of teachers to negotiate with their employers over the conditions of their employment has actually served to stimulate this interest. Certainly there are no significant differences in teaching conditions in New York, Pennsylvania, and Illinois, on the one hand, and in Wisconsin, Michigan, and Connecticut, on the other. Yet there have been scores of representation elections in the latter "covered" states, and many more-or-less comprehensive agreements have been negotiated, while there have been only a handful of elections in the former states which, as of the fall of 1966, had no enabling legislation. As more states pass legislation providing for collective bargaining rights for teachers, so too will the rivalry between the AFT and the NEA increase, and so too will the number of teachers covered by comprehensive collective agreements.

Ultimately the movement will level off, just as the organization of workers in private employment reached a plateau within a decade or so after the passage of the Wagner Act. In the meantime, it is only reasonable to expect that in most medium to large cities public school teachers will become organized as will those in suburban communities that fall within the big city ambient. In other areas, conditions will probably never be "ripe" for organization, and in still others we can expect that school board policies will hastily be rewritten to accommodate teacher demands, taking enough sting out of their grievances to make teachers feel that collective bargaining is unnecessary.

II

When workers in private employment began to agitate for collective bargaining rights in the 1930's, public policy was directed toward creating a balance between the bargaining power of employees and employers, which prior to that time had been weighted in favor of the employer. The concern then was equity or, as some observers put it, social justice. There was little concern that the quality of the industrial product would be affected by extending bargaining rights to workers. Prices might increase as they reflected improvements in wage scales and other benefits, which presumably collective bargaining would provide; but the market place, it was believed, would exercise a strong restraint on union demands. Unions have no interest in forcing employers out of business, nor are they unaware that it is the choices buyers make in the market, based in large part on price and quality of the product, that will ultimately determine the workers' economic welfare.

When it comes to collective bargaining in the public sector, and more particularly in public education, a different set of circumstances prevails. With the exception of the small minority who send their children to private schools, the parents of school-age children cannot shop around for the best educational buy. They are compelled by circumstances, partly legal, to send their children to schools in the local school district. They are also required, one should add, to support their schools with their tax dollars. They must, in other words, buy the product whether or not they think it's a good one.

Unlike industrial commodities, moreover, the quality of the educational product is almost exclusively determined by the quality of the educational employee. To be sure, the number of books in the school library, the equipment in the science laboratory, the curriculum, the imagination of the administrators, all have a bearing on the quality of the educational enterprise. But the fact remains that the most intimate and persuasive influence on the school child is his teacher. And it is the skill the teacher possesses and the dedication he shows that are the deciding factors in how well the child is educated.

Public policy regarding the employment arrangement in the schools transcends matters of equity or social justice for the employee, although in a democratic society this must always be an extremely important consideration. The public's paramount concern, after all, is in the educational welfare of its children. It is only natural then, when the public gets to the point of asking itself whether or not teachers should be allowed to bargain collectively over the conditions of their employment, it will ask whether this new arrangement will add to or detract from the quality of the educational program. Will the teachers be more competent or less? Will the administration be more or less free to make educational innovations? Will scarce tax dollars be allocated to those educational services that contribute best to the children's intellectual development?

Unquestionably collective bargaining will force changes in the allocation of educational resources. For while there is nothing in the bargaining arrangement that compels school boards to "give in" on any point, the fact is that once the board accepts the principle of good-faith bargaining it will find itself making certain changes in employment practices and, in some cases, educational policies. And when boards face teacher organizations imbued with a strong sense of militancy, willing and able to impose sanctions, secure mass resignations, or strike, one can anticipate that there will be substantial changes. One change seems to be certain — more tax money will be allocated to the schools and a large percentage of this increase will end up as higher salaries and other economic benefits for teachers. Occasionally these teacher benefits will come at the expense of other educational programs. The point is, however, that a determined teacher organization can extract from the community expenditures for education that the school administration and the school board, subject as they are to the more orderly political processes of budget approval, are powerless to secure.

There is, of course, a danger that collective bargaining will cause a disproportionate percentage of school funds to be spent on salaries and other related benefits (there is no comparable union or association that merely champions educational reforms), but the experience so far has not borne out this fear. What seems to have happened in those systems that have negotiated comprehensive collective agreements is that teaching conditions have improved and as a consequence of these improvements turnover rates have been lessened, recruitment has been made easier, the introduction of teacher aides to perform clerical and other subprofessional chores has provided teachers with more time to prepare lessons and consult with students, and class size, where this has been a feature of collective agreements, has been reduced. There also seems to have been a considerable improvement in morale, brought about not only by improved working conditions but also by the strong grievance procedures incorporated in most comprehensive agreements.

Surely the most critical problem in public education today is the shortage of qualified (certified) teachers. On the eve of opening school day in the fall of 1966, school officials in Illinois were trying to fill 21,000 teaching positions, New York State was short 15,000 certificated employees, and Missouri 1,600. Even in such a high-salaried state as California, the State Education Department had to grant 240 school districts permission to hire unqualified teachers on a provisional basis.[1] Tens of thousands of young men and women who had trained to become teachers had evidently decided after graduation that life would be more pleasant and more rewarding in non-teaching pursuits.

The juxtaposition of the improvements that have been or can be brought about by teacher collective bargaining with the current critical shortage of teachers points up the issue clearly. It may be, as we suggested earlier in this study, that both the NEA and AFT are placing too much emphasis on the employment relationship and relegating the professional role of teachers to a subsidiary position. But this shift in emphasis, even though motivated by self interest, can have a meritorious effect on the educational enterprise. If the current shortage of teachers has a great deal to do with the unhappy conditions that exist in most public school systems, and we strongly suspect it has, then it may be that only militant teacher action, including hardnosed collective bargaining, can create the employment conditions that will induce enough qualified young men and women to take up teaching as a life-time career. School boards alone have not been able to persuade the public to provide the wherewithal that would make public school teaching an attractive career for bright and energetic college graduates. It is conceivable that strong and determined teacher organizations can provide just the leverage needed.

III

A persuasive case can be made that collective bargaining is the only means by which teachers will achieve professional.status. This does not mean, however, that the bilateral determination of employment conditions does not present problems, some of them quite serious.

Teacher strikes will continue to be a problem. Even though the great

---

[1] *The Ann Arbor News,* August 30, 1966, p. 10, col. 1.

majority of teacher organizations may accept the result of the impasse-breaking procedures created by statutes or negotiated by the parties, there will still be some who will ignore them. Indeed, there seem to have been more work stoppages and threats thereof in the public schools between 1964 and 1966, the prime years of organizational activity and statute writing, than in any other two-year period in our history. And this in the face of the fact that such strikes are illegal in most states, either by statute or common law, and in some states — Michigan, for example — procedures have been developed to handle impasses by alternative means. Certainly there will be cases where teachers, knowing they have enough muscle to win the majority of their demands by striking, will not settle for half a loaf through arbitration or fact finding, even if the law says they must. No statute or bilaterally agreed-upon set of procedures can *guarantee* that there will be no disruption of educational services.

Perhaps as important as the disruptive effect of these occasional strikes is the psychological influence they may have on school children. We expect our teachers to teach respect for law and order, not merely as a textbook or academic exercise, but by example. If teachers do strike in violation of the law and gain certain concessions thereby, this lesson in *Realpolitik* will hardly be lost on their students.

But it is easy to exaggerate the disruptive and psychological effect these strikes can have. And to introduce two countering factors, if we may extrapolate from the immediate past, it is probably safe to predict that teacher strikes will be short in duration (two or three days) and that by no means all teachers will go out (elementary schools continued to operate almost normally during many strikes of recent years).

Although strikes and strike threats may be the most worrisome aspect of collective bargaining in the schools, there are other, less dramatic, problems that may arise from a formalized employment relationship. Grievance procedures, for example, which most students of employee relations would argue should be an essential feature of almost any employment relationship, can and have been abused. Sometimes the grievance machinery is used as a political weapon to bring non-members and dissident members into line. Administrators can be intimidated by teachers' threats to process grievances, and there have already been cases where school principals have against their better judgment made assignments of certain teachers to special classes or to a particular type of extra duty only because they wanted to avoid a troublesome grievance. One can sympathize with teachers who have labored under a system characterized by petty tyranny or favoritism, and it is not difficult to understand why they should want to bring about more "democracy at the work place" through a strong grievance machinery. But at the same time one can sympathize with administrators who are charged with the responsibility of allocating human resources in the most efficient way possible and are frustrated in their efforts by the "abuse" of a contract provision.

Indeed, if one can draw a parallel between collective bargaining in the schools and what has happened in private industry, it becomes apparent that one of the most serious problems school management faces in formalized employee arrangements is the diminution of administrative flexibility. The administration's transfer and promotion policies are sometimes at loggerheads with the security aspirations of individual teachers; the superintendent's desire to make educational innovations can run counter to the wishes of teachers to retain the more familiar and more comfortable work patterns. It is true that school boards, administrators, and teachers constitute an educational team with a wide range of common interests. But it is also true that when it comes to working conditions they divide into employers and employees with significant areas of conflicting interests. Collective bargaining is not designed to remove these differences but to establish rules of · the game whereby the means for the resolution of conflict may be institutionalized.

Another problem that can be exacerbated by collective bargaining is that of dislodging incompetent teachers from the classrooms. Teachers are probably overprotected by present tenure laws, however inequitably rewarded under existing salary schedules. And now that both the NEA and the AFT are locked in competition for teacher allegiance, it is unlikely that either organization will find it politically expedient to fight less for the incompetents and time-servers than for able teachers. The danger is that the formalized employment arrangement will freeze into school systems all the inequities of former personnel practices and preserve few of their virtues. While collective bargaining may one day be successful in raising salaries to a point where enough highly competent men and women will be attracted to the field, we shall in the meantime, unless some form of merit pay is introduced and tenure restrictions are modified, be faced with no alternative but to pay these same high salaries to the many teachers who don't even "earn" what they are presently paid.

IV

Serious as they are, it may be that the problems mentioned above will be short run. Probably within a decade or so the institutional posturing

124

of the two major teacher organizations will have been taken care of by merger or some kind of "no-raiding" agreement. Certainly the novelty will wear off, and leaders of the two teacher organizations will no longer feel they must flex their muscles in quite the present fashion. By the same token, one can expect that school board members will learn that they can no longer remain intransigent, invoking pleas of poverty, management rights, or sovereignty in the face of legitimate teacher demands.

Also, if the present movement to improve the status of teachers by collective action is successful, if, in other words, teachers should come close to realizing what they seem to be striving toward, the concern over purely employment matters will decline. Then, perhaps, we can get on with the business of worrying about how best to educate children.

Teachers have always sought professional status. Ironically, they may achieve this status by first learning how to act like militant trade unionists, thus securing the economic base that will allow them to concentrate on professional problems. Whether they succeed in making this transition or merely continue to pursue the trade union route is a matter almost beyond conjecture. The undisputed fact, however, is that teachers are beginning to assert a much greater influence on how our schools are run, and we are witnessing just the beginnings of this movement. Nor is there likely to be any turning back. If teacher leaders and school officials learn to use this development wisely, it may prove to be the most therapeutic educational development of this century. If they do not, it may freeze into our system, more firmly than ever before, those personnel practices that can only lead to educational mediocrity. In either case, a rather profound change is taking place in the guardianship of public education.

Appendix

Representative provisions in two comprehensive teacher – school-board agreements, negotiated by affiliates of the American Federation of Teachers and the National Education Association, are set forth below. The purpose is twofold: (1) to acquaint the reader with the form and some of the contents of such collective agreements; and (2) to demonstrate the degree of similarity that may obtain between contracts negotiated by the two competing teacher organizations. (For further commentary on the similarity between contracts negotiated by the Association and the Union, see pages 38–41 supra.)

A Comparison of Representative Provisions of AFT and NEA Agreements

New Haven Teachers League (Connecticut Education Association, NEA) and New Haven Board of Education; Boston Teachers Union, Local 66 (AFT) and School Committee of City of Boston.

New Haven	Boston
(Association)	(Federation)

CLASS SIZE / CLASS SIZE

New Haven (Association)	Boston (Federation)
Wherever feasible under the circumstances (e.g., availability of staff and facilities), in both elementary schools (including kindergarten) and secondary schools (junior and senior high):	The Committee and the Union recognize the desirability of achieving optimum teaching-learning conditions by assuring workable class size. To this end the Committee recognizes it is desirable to attempt to reach the following class size maxima:
1. No regular class shall have more than thirty pupils.	20 pupils in classes of accademically talented or slow academic achievers
2. No Special Education class shall have more than twenty pupils. The composition and size of such classes shall be in accordance with State Board of Education policy.	20 pupils in industrial arts classes
3. Classes containing concentrations of disadvantaged pupils shall be reduced in size as rapidly as practicable to a number which permits optimum learning opportunities for such pupils.	12 pupils in industrial arts classes composed of special class students
4. No teacher shall, at any given time, be assigned the class responsibility, regardless of the size of his classes, for more than 125 pupils.	To achieve these class size targets the Union and the Committee agree that the following class size maxima for the 1966–67 school year shall be in effect:
	28 in kindergarten through grade 6
	32 in grades 7–12

The foregoing standards are subject to modification for educational purposes such as the avoidance of split-grade classes or half-classes or specialized or experimental instruction (e.g., music, team teaching, typing classes, physical education).

An appropriate number of regular teachers shall be hired to make possible the aforementioned class size maxima for the 1966–67 school year.

In the event that it is necessary to assign a teacher to a class which exceeds the maximum size, the Headmaster or Principal shall upon receipt of written request by the teacher or the Union state reasons in writing to the teacher and the Union and the Associate Superintendent of Personnel. Such a statement of specific reasons shall be available for examination by the Union in the Office of the Associate Superintendent of Personnel and the office of the Principal or Headmaster.

An acceptable reason for exceeding the maximum class size may be any of the following:

(a) There is no space available and no portable unit can be obtained to permit scheduling of any additional classes or class in order to reduce class size.

(b) Conformity to the class size objective would result in placing additional classes on short time schedule.

(c) Conformity to the class size objective would result in the organization of half-classes.

(d) A class larger than the maximum is necessary or desirable in order to provide for specialized or experimental instruction, or for the instruction of the gifted.

(e) It is educationally unsound.

PROMOTIONS

A. All vacancies in promotional positions caused by death, retirement, discharge, resignation, or by the creation of a new promotional position shall be filled pursuant to the following procedure:

PROMOTIONS

A circular by the Superintendent shall be sent to all schools whenever vacancies occur or are about to occur on higher positions or more desirable positions within the bargaining unit or on levels above the bargain-

1. Such vacancies shall be adequately publicized, including a notice in every school (by posting, through the Superintendent's bulletin, or otherwise) as far in advance of the date of filling such vacancy as possible (ordinarily, at least 30 days in advance and in no event less than two weeks in advance).

2. Said notice of vacancy shall clearly set forth the qualifications for the position.

3. Teachers who desire to apply for such vacancies shall file their applications in writing with the Office of the Superintendent within the time limit specified in the notice.

4. Such vacancy shall be filled on the basis of fitness for the vacant post, provided, however, that where two or more applicants are substantially equal in fitness, the applicant with the greatest amount of seniority in the New Haven school system shall be given preference.

B. Promotional positions are defined as follows: positions paying a salary differential and/or positions on the administrator-supervisory level, including but not limited to, positions as assistant superintendent, supervisor, assistant supervisor, director, assistant director, principal, assistant principal, department chairman, counselor, and administrative assistant.

C. All vacancies (as defined above in the case of promotional positions) for specialists and/or special project teachers shall also be filled pursuant to the procedure set forth in Paragraph A above.

D. All appointments to the aforesaid vacancies and openings shall be made without regard to age, race, creed, color, religion, nationality, sex or marital status.

ing unit, or when new positions of comparable status are to be established. Notice shall be posted on the appropriate bulletin board by the Principal, Head Master or Director. Copies shall be sent to the Union.

Qualifications, requirements, duties, salary and other pertinent information shall be categorically set forth in the foregoing notices.

All applications shall be considered.

All applications shall be in writing and shall set forth the position for which the applicant is to be considered. Reasonable time shall be allowed for such submission of applications. (A minimum of 10 school days.) A minimum of 10 school days after notice from Board of Examiners shall be given to file qualifications.

Notice must be given to all personnel at least 6 months in advance of any change in qualifications for any positions set forth in the first paragraph of this Article.

E. Notwithstanding the foregoing, vacancies may be filled without following the foregoing procedure when it is impracticable because the need to fill the vacancy has arisen during the summer months.

GRIEVANCE PROCEDURE

The purpose of the following grievance procedure shall be to settle equitably at the lowest possible administrative level issues which may arise from time to time with respect to the salaries and working conditions of teachers provided for in this Agreement. The Board and the League agree that these proceedings shall be kept as informal and confidential as may be appropriate at any level of the procedure. The Board also agrees to make available to any aggrieved person and/or his representative all data not privileged under law which is within the possession of the Board and which bears on the issues raised by the grievance.

1. *Definitions.*

A "grievance" is hereby defined to mean (a) a complaint by a teacher or a group of teachers based upon an alleged violation of or variation from the provisions of this Agreement, or the interpretation, meaning or application thereof, or (b) that the Board failed to act in good faith in exercising its judgment or discretion as provided for in Article I, Section 8 of this Agreement — i.e., that it acted arbitrarily, capriciously or without rational basis in fact, or (c) that the League has acted unreasonably in withholding its approval where called for under this Agreement. An "aggrieved person" is a person or group of persons making such a complaint. A "party in interest" is a person or group of

GRIEVANCE PROCEDURE

It is the declared objective of the parties to encourage prompt resolution of grievances. The parties recognize the importance of prompt and equitable disposition of any complaint at the lowest organizational level possible. Teachers subject to this Agreement shall not suffer a loss of pay for time spent in conferring and meeting on a grievance; provided, however, that conferences and meetings will not normally take place during periods when the teachers involved have classroom duties, except as otherwise provided herein. Any person(s) or the Union shall have the right to present a grievance and have it promptly considered on its merits.

A. *Definition.*

A "grievance" shall mean a complaint (1) that there has been as to a teacher a violation, misinterpretation or inequitable application of any of the provisions of this agreement or (2) that a teacher has been treated unfairly or inequitably by reason of any act or condition which is contrary to established policy or practice governing or affecting employees, except that the term "grievance" shall not apply to any matter as to which the Committee is without authority to act. As used in this article, the term "person" or "teacher" shall mean also a group of teachers having the same grievance.

persons (including the Board or any of its representatives) who might be required to take action or against whom action might be taken in order to resolve the complaint.

2. Procedure.

Since it is important that grievances be processed as rapidly as possible, the number of days indicated at each level should be considered as maximum and every effort should be made to expedite the process. The time limits specified may, however, be extended by mutual agreement.

In the event a grievance is filed on or after June 1 which, if left unresolved until the beginning of the following school year, could result in irreparable harm to a party in interest, the time limits set forth herein shall be reduced so that the grievance procedure may be exhausted prior to the end of the school term or as soon thereafter as is practicable.

Level One.

A teacher with a grievance shall first discuss it with his immediate supervisor and/or principal, either directly or with the League's School Representative, with the objective of resolving the matter informally.

Level Two.

(a) in the event that the aggrieved person is not satisfied with the disposition of his grievance at Level One, or in the event that no decision has been rendered within ten (10) school days after presentation of the grievance, he may file the grievance in writing with the Chairman of the League's Committee on Professional Rights and Responsibilities within five (5) school days after the decision at Level One or fifteen

B. *Adjustment of Grievances.*

Grievances of employees within the bargaining unit shall be presented and adjusted in the following manner:

1. *General Procedures.*

(a) School Level (Step 1)

A teacher or his Union representative may either orally or in writing, present a grievance to the Principal, Head Master or Director within a reasonable time, normally within thirty (30) school days after knowledge by the teacher of the facts giving rise to the act or condition which is the basis of his complaint.

The teacher and the Principal, Head Master or Director of the school shall confer on the grievance with a view to arriving at a mutually satisfactory resolution of the complaint. At the conference, the teacher may present the grievance personally or he may be represented by a Union representative; but where the teacher is represented he must be present. Whenever a grievance is presented to the Principal, Head Master, or Director by the teacher personally, the Principal, Head Master or Director shall give the Union representative the opportunity to be present and state the views of the Union.

The Principal, Head Master or Director shall communicate his decision orally or in writing to the aggrieved teacher and to any Union representative who participated in this step within ten (10) school days after receiving the complaint.

(b) Associate Superintendent of Personnel Level (Step 2)

If the grievance is not resolved at Step 1, the aggrieved teacher or the Union may appeal by forwarding the grievance in writing to the Asso-

(15) school days after the grievance was presented, whichever is sooner. Within five (5) school days after receiving the written grievance, the Chairman shall refer it in writing to the Superintendent of Schools.

(b) The Superintendent shall represent the Board at this level of the grievance procedure. Within ten (10) school days after receipt of the written grievance by the Superintendent, the Superintendent or his designee shall meet with the aggrieved person in an effort to resolve it.

(c) If a teacher does not file a grievance in writing with the Chairman of the Committee on PR&R and the written grievance is not forwarded to the Superintendent within thirty (30) school days after the teacher knew or should have known of the act or condition on which the grievance is based, then the grievance shall have been waived. A dispute as to whether a grievance has been waived under this paragraph shall be subject to arbitration pursuant to Level Four.

Level Three.

In the event that the aggrieved person is not satisfied with the disposition of his grievance at Level Two, or in the event no decision has been rendered within ten (10) school days after he has first met with the Superintendent or his designee, he may file the grievance in writing with the Chairman of the Committee on PR&R within five (5) school days after a decision by the Superintendent, or fifteen (15) school days after he has first met with the Superintendent, whichever is sooner. Within five (5) school days after receiving the written grievance, the Chairman of the Committee on PR&R

ciate Superintendent in Charge of Personnel within ten (10) school days after he has received the Step 1 decision. The appeal shall include:

a. Name and position of grievant;

b. A statement of the grievance and the facts involved;

c. The corrective action requested;

d. Name of Union representative at Step 1, if any;

e. Signature(s) of grievant(s) or Union representative.

The Associate Superintendent in Charge of Personnel will arrange for a conference with the aggrieved teacher and his Union representatives, if any. The aggrieved teacher and the Union representatives shall be given at least two (2) school days' notice of the conference. The aggrieved teacher shall be present at the conference, except that he need not attend where it is mutually agreed that no facts are in dispute and that the sole question before the Associate Superintendent in Charge of Personnel is one of interpretation of a provision of this Agreement or of what is established policy or practice. The Head Master, Principal or Director may be present at this conference and state his views. The Associate Superintendent in charge of Personnel shall issue a written decision on the grievance as soon as possible, but not later than seventeen (17) school days after the receipt of the appeal. A copy will be sent to the aggrieved person and the Union.

(c) Superintendent of Schools (Step 3)

The decision of the foregoing step may be appealed in writing by the teacher or the Union to the Superintendent of Schools within fifteen (15) school days after the decision of the Associate Superintendent in

132

shall refer it to the Board. Within ten (10) school days after receiving the written Grievance, the Board shall meet with the aggrieved person for the purpose of resolving the grievance.

Level Four.

(a) In the event that the aggrieved person is not satisfied with the disposition of his grievance at Level Three, or in the event no decision has been rendered within ten (10) school days after he has first met with the Board, he may, within five (5) school days after a decision by the Board or fifteen (15) school days after he has first met with the Board, whichever is sooner, request in writing the Committee on PR&R to submit his grievance to arbitration. If the Committee on PR&R determines that the grievance is meritorious and submitting it for arbitration is in the best interest of the New Haven school system, it may by written notice to the Board submit the grievance to arbitration within fifteen (15) school days after receipt of a request by the aggrieved person.

(b) Within ten (10) school days after such written notice of arbitration, representatives of the Board and the Committee on PR&R shall agree upon and select an arbitrator or arbitrators. If the parties cannot agree upon an arbitrator or arbitrators at this meeting, a request for a list of five (5) arbitrators shall be made to the American Arbitration Association by the Committee on PR&R. Beginning with the League acting through the Committee on PR&R, the League and the Board shall alternately strike a name from the list until only one (1) person remains, who shall be the arbitrator.

Charge of Personnel has been received. The Superintendent of Schools or his designated representative shall meet with the aggrieved teacher and the Union representatives. The aggrieved teacher and the Union representatives will receive at least two (2) school days' notice of the meeting and an opportunity to be heard. The Head Master, Principal or Director and Associate Superintendent in Charge of Personnel may be present at the meeting and state their views. The Superintendent or his designated representative shall communicate his written decision together with supporting reasons to the aggrieved teacher and to the Union as soon as possible but not later than seventeen (17) school days after receipt of the appeal.

(d) The Committee (Step 4)

The decision of the foregoing step may be appealed in writing by the teacher or the Union to the Committee for review within thirty (30) days after the decision of the Superintendent has been received.

The Committee shall meet with the aggrieved teacher and/or the Union Representatives. The aggrieved teacher and the Union Representatives will receive at least two (2) school days' notice of the meeting and an opportunity to be heard. The Superintendent, or his designated representative, the Associate Superintendent in Charge of Personnel, the Principal, Head Master or Director may be present at the meeting and state their views.

2. *Initiation of Grievances or Complaints Filed by the Union at Steps 2 or 3.*

(a) Grievances arising from the action of officials other than the Principal, Head Master or Director

(c) The arbitrator so selected shall confer with representatives of the Board and the Committee on PR&R and hold hearings promptly and, unless extended by mutual agreement, shall issue his decision not later than twenty (20) days from the date of the closing of the hearings or, if oral hearings have been waived, then from the date the final statements and proofs are submitted to him. The arbitrator's decision shall be in writing and shall set forth his findings of fact, reasoning and conclusions on the issues submitted. The arbitrator shall be without power or authority to make any decision which requires the commission of an act prohibited by law or which is violative of the terms of this Agreement. The decision of the arbitrator shall be submitted to the Board and to the League and, subject to law, shall be final and binding, provided that the arbitrator shall not usurp the functions of the Board or the proper exercise of its judgment and discretion under law and this Agreement.

(d) The costs for the services of the arbitrator including per diem expenses, if any, and actual and necessary travel and subsistence expenses, shall be borne equally by the Board and the League.

3. *Rights of Teachers to Representation.*

a. No reprisals of any kind shall be taken by any party to this Agreement against any party in interest, any witness, any member of the Committee on PR&R or any other participant in the grievance procedure by reason of such participation.

b. Any party in interest may be represented at all stages of this may be initiated with and processed in accordance with the provisions of Step 2 of this grievance procedure. Where the action is initiated by the Superintendent of Schools, the grievance may be filed at Step 3.

(b) Conferences held under this procedure at Step 2 or Step 3 shall be conducted at a time and place which will afford a fair and reasonable opportunity for all persons entitled to be present to attend. When such conferences are held during day school hours, all persons who participate shall be excused with pay.

3. *Salary and Leave Grievances.*

The following grievances shall be presented directly to the Associate Superintendent in Charge of Personnel at Step 2 and in accordance with the time requirements for filing as set forth in Step 1.

(a) A grievance alleging that the person was placed on the wrong step of the salary schedule.

(b) A grievance alleging the person's wages were improperly paid.

(c) A grievance alleging the person was improperly denied an increment.

(d) A grievance alleging the person's absence deduction was improperly calculated.

(e) A grievance alleging the person was improperly denied a sabbatical leave.

(f) A grievance alleging the person was improperly denied a leave of absence without pay.

4. (a) The time limits specified in any step of this procedure may be extended, in any specific instance, by mutual agreement.

grievance procedure by a person of his own choosing, except that he may not be represented by a representative or by an officer of any teacher organization other than the League. When a teacher is not represented by the League, the League shall have the right to be present and to state its views at all stages of this grievance procedure.

4. *Miscellaneous.*

a. If, in the judgment of the Committee on PR&R, a grievance affects a group or class of teachers, the Committee on PR&R may submit such grievance in writing to the Superintendent directly and the processing of such grievance shall be commenced at Level Two. The Committee on PR&R may process such a grievance through all levels of the procedure even though the aggrieved persons do not wish to do so.

b. Decisions rendered at Levels Two and Three of the grievance procedure shall be in writing setting forth the decision and the reasons therefor and shall be promptly transmitted to all parties in interest and to the Chairman of the Committee on PR&R. Decisions rendered at Level Four shall be in accordance with the procedures hereinbefore set out therefor.

c. Forms for filing and processing grievances and other documents necessary under the procedure shall be prepared by the Superintendent and given appropriate distribution so as to facilitate operation of the grievance procedure. All documents, communications and records dealing with the processing of a grievance shall be filed separately from the personnel files of the participants.

(b) A grievance filed in an inappropriate step of the grievance procedure will be considered as properly filed but the time limits for answering the grievance shall not begin until the grievance is referred to the appropriate step.

5. In the event that the immediacy of a complaint requires a teacher to meet with his Principal or Head Master suddenly (on a non-scheduled occasion) he shall be allowed to have his Union Representative present at the meeting provided he first makes this request of the Principal or Head Master.

6. A failure by a teacher or the Union to process the grievance from one step to the next step within the time limits provided for will result in a disposition of this grievance unfavorable to the grievant, and conversely, a failure of a representative of the Committee responsible to answer a grievance at any of the steps of the grievance procedure to make sure an answer within the time limits provided for will result in a disposition of the grievance favorable to the grievant.

C. The Union shall furnish the Committee with a list of its officers, and authorized Union Representatives, and shall as soon as possible notify the Committee in writing of any changes. No Union Representative shall be recognized by the Committee except those designated in writing by the Union.

ARBITRATION

A grievance which was not resolved at Step 4 under the grievance procedure may be submitted by the Union to arbitration. The arbitration may be initiated by filing with the Committee and the American

(d) The procedure set forth above shall be the sole and exclusive remedy available to an aggrieved person hereunder.

(e) Failure at any step of this procedure to communicate the decision on a grievance within the specified time limits shall permit the aggrieved employee to proceed to the next step. Failure at any step of this procedure to appeal a grievance to the next step within the specified time limits shall be deemed to be acceptance of the decision rendered at that step.

(f) Any decision, course of conduct or other action which becomes the subject of a grievance shall not be stayed pending the processing of the grievance except with the written consent of the Superintendent or the Board, which consent shall not be unreasonably withheld. A decision at any level of the procedure in favor of the aggrieved person, however, may provide appropriate restitution or other remedy for the period during which the grievance was suffered.

Arbitration Association a request for arbitration. The notice shall be filed within sixty (60) school days after denial of the grievance at Step 4 under the Grievance Procedure. The voluntary labor arbitration rules of the American Arbitration Association shall apply to the proceeding.

The arbitrator shall issue his written decision not later than thirty (30) days after the date of the close of the hearings or, if oral hearings have been waived, then from the date of transmitting the final statements and proofs to the arbitrator. The decision of the arbitrator will be accepted as final by the parties to the disputes and both will abide by it.

The Committee agrees that it will apply to all substantially similar situations the decision of an arbitrator sustaining a grievance and the Union agrees that it will not bring or continue, and that it will not represent any employee in any grievance which is substantially similar to a grievance denied by the decision of an arbitrator. The arbitrator's fee will be shared equally by the parties to the dispute.

Index

139

E